fresh from the
freezer

fresh from the freezer

100 delicious freezer-friendly recipes

Ghillie James

Photography by Tara Fisher

KYLE BOOKS

Dedicated to Eva, Alice, Charlie, Leo, Florence and Isla.
With my love x

First published in Great Britain in 2011 by
Kyle Books
23 Howland Street
London, W1T 4AY
general.enquiries@kylebooks.com
www.kylebooks.com

ISBN: 978-0-85783-002-9

Text © 2011 Ghillie James
Design © 2011 Kyle Books
Photographs © 2011 Tara Fisher

Ghillie James is hereby identified as the author of this work in accordance
with Section 77 of the Copyright, Designs and Patents Act 1988.

Editor: Catharine Robertson
Designer: Lizzie Ballantyne
Photographer: Tara Fisher
Food stylist: Debbie Miller
Props stylist: Liz Belton
Copy editor: Anne Newman
Index: Helen Snaith
Production: Gemma John, Nic Jones and Sheila Smith

A Cataloguing in Publication record for this title is available from the
British Library.

Colour reproduction by Media Image in Italy
Printed and bound in China by Toppan Leefung Printing Ltd.

contents

introduction

You only have to wander down the frozen food aisle of your local supermarket to realise that freezing has moved on in leaps and bounds over the past few years. Battered fish sticks and suspect chicken pies with no discernible filling have been moved aside to make way for soufflés, risottos and char-grilled aubergines. For me this area of the supermarket was always for convenience only – frozen peas and ice cream for busy days when I had no time to cook. Now, however, I find myself ogling the canapés and tarts, scallops and summer fruits, held back only by my purse strings.

But has our home freezing gone the same way? When there's a glut of fresh fruit and veg in the garden that tastes at its best, are we turning berries into ice cream, or cooking and freezing a stash of fresh tomato soup for weekend lunches or an ice-cube tray full of homemade Thai green curry paste for busy days and hungry children? Or what about preparing a batch of lamb tagine and a selection of frozen vodkas to pull out when friends pop over for an impromptu Friday night in front of a DVD? With so many time-stretched, nutrition-savvy and budget-conscious families, it's the freezer, not the fridge that should be our best friend in the kitchen.

Food from the freezer needn't be dull, stodgy or bland. Clear out your freezer, defrost it, then fill it with your favourite kinds of food. Whether that is a fantastic homemade curry sauce and ice cream to save on a tempting takeaway, prepare-ahead canapés and puddings for a hectic Christmas, biscuit dough ready to bake or homemade pizzas ready to top when you have children to entertain on a rainy Sunday afternoon.

A freezer is *the* kitchen appliance for those who want to save money. You can make double when foods are cheaper or in season, buy produce on offer and, most importantly, freeze your leftovers rather than throw them away. From breadcrumbs to egg yolks, there are heaps of leftovers that are suitable for freezing, as well as mountains of things to do with them.

The freezer should especially be a new mum's best friend. Supermarket baby food has moved on from long-life jars of unrecognisable gloop to incredibly nutritious organic pots and sachets – but sadly available at incredibly high prices. I use them myself, when we are going away for a weekend or on holiday, so that I can guarantee that I have something on hand when arriving at a holiday house and my one-year-old daughter decides she wants her lunch NOW! However, I can't justify using them everyday, nor have I time to lovingly prepare individual meals that each take an hour to make and then spoon into pots. With my second child, I've worked out a way of making baby purées that can be quick and easy – and, I think, more nutritious as well. I've also devised some toddler food that will please the parents, too – and, no, it's not just cottage pie and pasta bake!

I hope that *Fresh from the Freezer* inspires you, gives you some handy tips and helps you to make the most of fruit and veg in abundance. I also hope that it makes your busy life easier – it certainly has helped mine

ten reasons to freeze

1. Buy produce such as meat in bulk, and make the most of good offers and deals, then just use it as you need it.

2. Prepare and freeze local, in-season produce when it tastes at its best and costs less. You can then enjoy your favourite foods year round, without the air miles.

3. Get ahead and prepare for entertaining in advance to prevent last-minute hard work.

4. Use half a bag of something and just freeze the rest – freezing is ideal if you are cooking for one or trying to keep fussy-eaters happy.

5. Freezing acts as a natural preservative, so you can enjoy your favourite things in their natural state, rather than bottled or jarred.

6. Get your 'five a day' with ease – frozen foods often contain more vitamins and minerals than fresh, as produce can be frozen immediately, before it has time to deteriorate. Frozen peas contain up to 40 per cent more vitamin C than two-day-old fresh ones, for example.

7. No need to chuck leftovers anymore – save time and money and freeze them. (See page 13 for ideas.)

8. Save time by cooking straight from the freezer instead of shopping on the way home from work.

9. Make recipes in batches when you have time and use them up in quick recipes when you don't.

10. Take the stress out of cooking for babies and toddlers with cubes and pots in the freezer that take minutes to reheat.

(F)   Freezing

(D)   Defrosting

(R)   Reheating

(C)   Cooking

(S)   Serving

freezing – the rules

Always freeze produce and recipes when they are at their freshest – don't be tempted to freeze something that's about to go off – it won't taste good once defrosted and cooked!

Never refreeze anything when still in the same state as when you defrosted it, ie. raw or cooked. So, if you defrost a raw chicken or some mince it must be cooked before you can refreeze it. If you've defrosted something cooked then you can't refreeze it again.

Always make sure that you wrap things well, whether in a double layer of foil, in a freezer bag or lidded container – it will protect the food, preserve the flavour and prevent anything getting freezer burn.

If freezing liquids, always leave a little extra space at the top of the container, bag or bottle to allow for expansion.

Freeze things as quickly as possible – use the fast-freeze button on your freezer if you have one.

Don't overcrowd the freezer as it won't work as efficiently.

Cool food as quickly as possible once cooked, and freeze it only when completely cool.

Stick to recommended storage times (see page 12).

Open-freeze 'wet' foods such as sausages, raspberries or iced cakes on a tray, uncovered, in a single layer to prevent them sticking together or ruining. Once frozen, transfer to a bag or container.

storing and thawing

I'm not going to start advising on which is the best freezer to buy, as to be honest I don't have a clue! However, I have thoroughly researched the latest in boxes, bags and labels to help you freeze your food effectively, use up the minimum of space and keep it at its optimum quality.

Take it from me, there's nothing more annoying than digging out a cake or casserole from the freezer that has either been knocked about or damaged from cold air, which causes freezer burn (dehydration patches on the food). Careful wrapping and storage will increase the freezer life of food substantially, so it really isn't a waste of money to buy some strong good-quality freezer boxes and bags, and most importantly some labels and a freezer pen.

Boxes and bags

There are lots out there, from old ice-cream containers to snazzy lockable lidded boxes. Make sure that the lids are tight fitting and bear in mind that if you buy a few of the same shape, they will stack well and therefore take up less space. If you are buying boxes especially for use in the freezer, it's worth checking that they are both dishwasher and microwave-proof. I use boxes for storing cakes, meringues, sausage rolls and any other food items that might get damaged if bashed about a bit. I also freeze small quantities of sauces, such as apple and bread sauce, in plastic boxes or pots so that I can defrost then reheat them in the box in the microwave.

There are now some incredible freezer bags available. Some have zips, which makes it easy to dip in for a handful then quickly zip shut – they are great for fruit, vegetables or breadcrumbs. I also highly recommend buying some of the gusseted freezer bags that are specially designed for storing soups and sauces – they stand up easily and have extremely strong zips to prevent spillages. Having some of these instead of boxes of soups and sauces will save you lots of space.

Labelling

Buy strong labels that are designed to go in the freezer, which will prevent the frustration of trying to establish what's in a box at the bottom of the freezer when the label has dropped off! For bags, use a freezer marker pen (write on the bag before you fill it!). I tend to write what it is, how many portions, when it was made and, if I need reminding, the use-by date.

Thawing frozen food

It is hard to be precise with thawing times as it very much depends on the type of container you have frozen the food in – food in a thick metal container will take longer to defrost than food in a china or plastic one – and the quantity you have made. My suggestions are, therefore, just a guide. The safest place to defrost food is always in the fridge, where it will defrost slowly and remain cold once thawed. However, as a large container or casserole for eight could take up to two days to defrost in a very cold fridge, there is no harm in starting things off in a cool place for a few hours, then transferring it to the fridge to finish off. But make sure that the place you choose is cool – don't leave food out to defrost in the height of summer near a window, especially if it contains meat, fish, dairy produce or eggs! You can also use the microwave for defrosting and reheating, just make sure it is piping hot and you eat it straight away.

Food Standards Agency Advice

Cooking food from frozen

The FSA always advise that any manufacturer's guidelines for the storage and cooking of foods should be adhered to. Commercially produced foods that are sold to be cooked from frozen will have had the cooking instructions determined by thorough testing. The important thing when cooking most meats such as poultry, minced/chopped meat (e.g. burgers and sausages) and rolled joints is to ensure that it is thoroughly cooked until steaming hot throughout, with the centre of the meat reaching a temperature of 70°C for 2 minutes or equivalent. You should also ensure that when you cut into these meats, no pinkness remains and any juices run clear. Be aware that it will take longer to reheat directly from frozen than to reheat food that has been thoroughly defrosted.

Freezing and re-freezing food

The FSA advise that frozen food should not be refrozen once it has defrosted without cooking thoroughly first. This is because thawing may not always be done carefully allowing multiplication of potentially harmful bacteria. If the meat is refrozen these bacteria may survive and there will be a further opportunity for bacteria to multiply when the meat is thawed again. Whilst cooking should destroy any potentially harmful bacteria present, the higher levels of bacteria in the raw meat will increase the risk of cross contamination in the kitchen. Refreezing, defrosting and reheating of food should not be done more than once. There should be no problem with freezing and reheating cooked food containing an ingredient that has previously been frozen or cooked. As the food will be cooked thoroughly as part of a dish, it should be fine to freeze this dish and reheat, but only once.

Storage times

Here's a helpful guide to maximum storage times for freezer-friendly foods. Label and date things when you freeze them to prevent the risk of leaving foods in for too long (or they will lose their flavour). Remember, too, that the key to successful freezing is to wrap things well (see page 10).

Raw meat and fish

(Larger joints of meat will keep longer than smaller cuts.)

Bacon: 3–4 months
Beef: 8–12 months
Chicken: 8–12 months
Duck: 6 months
Game: 12 months
Lamb: 6–8 months
Mince: 3–4 months
Oily fish: 2–3 months
Pork: 4–6 months
Prawns and scallops: 3–4 months
Sausages: 3–4 months
Smoked fish: 2 months
White fish: 4 months

Cooked foods

Baby purées: 2 months
Biscuits and flapjacks: 4 months
Bread: 3 months
Butter: 6 months (best to freeze
  unsalted)
Cakes: 3 months
Casseroles, soups and sauces:
  3 months
Cheese, hard: 6–8 months
Cheese, soft: 3 months
Cooked meat (e.g. ham pieces):
  1–2 months
Cream: 3 months
Eggs, raw, yolks/white: 12 months
Meringues and pavlovas: 1 month
Mousses, ice cream and sorbet:
  2 months

Pancakes and Yorkshire puddings:
  2 months
Pastry: 3 months
Stock: 6 months
Tarts, quiches, sausage rolls and
  pies: 3 months

Fruit and vegetables

Apples, peeled, cored and sliced:
  4–6 months, open freeze slices,
  then bag
Asparagus, blanched: 12 months,
  cook from frozen
Beans, blanched: 6–8 months, cook
  from frozen
Butternut squash, raw: 12 months,
  open freeze, then bag, cook from
  frozen
Chips: up to 18 months
Corn on the cob: 6–8 months, cook
  from frozen
Herbs, fresh: 4–6 months
Rhubarb, raw, chopped: 12 months,
  cook from frozen
Seville oranges: 6–8 months
Stone fruit, halved and stoned: 12
  months, unstoned: 3 months, cook
  from frozen
Summer berries: 12 months, open
  freeze (strawberries need to be
  puréed before freezing), defrost
  and use, or cook from frozen
Tomatoes, halved: 6–8 months, open
  freeze, then bag, use only for
  cooking, or grill tomato halves

top leftovers to freeze

These suggestions for leftover food items to throw in the freezer and use at a later date have been accumulated by friends and family, all of whom have frozen leftovers with great success over the years!

Batter – for pancakes or Yorkshire puddings, for example (see pages 29 and 30), try freezing uncooked in small pots

Bread – turn day-old bread into crumbs (see page 23) then freeze in bags and use from frozen

Buttercream icing

Cheese –

Hard cheese – can become more crumbly after freezing though, so use for crumbling into recipes, or grate prior to freezing, then freeze in bags and use from frozen

Soft-rinded cheese, such as Brie or Camembert

Cooked vegetables – add to a pot of soup or bubble and squeak

Cream (not single) – good for sauces but not for whipping

Egg whites – freeze in pots or bags (make sure to note number of eggs), defrost and use as fresh

Egg yolks – use an ice-cube tray, sprinkle with salt or sugar, defrost then use in sweet or savoury recipes

Elderflower cordial

Fruit juice

Gravy

Herbs – chop then freeze (herbs that bruise, for example basil and tarragon, can be chopped and frozen in oil)

Homemade barbecue sauce

Lasagne or pasta bake – freeze leftovers as individual portions

Lemons, oranges and limes – slice and open freeze on a tray before putting into a bag

Mashed potato

Meat jelly from roasting chicken or turkey – pour off the fat and freeze the leftover jelly in cubes, defrost, then use to add to casseroles and gravies

Milk

Pasta or curry sauce from a jar

Pastry

Pesto – freeze in ice-cube trays

Roast chicken carcass – make stock at a later date

Roast meats, such as chicken or ham – shred or cube then bag, defrost and use

Tinned tomatoes

Wine – freeze in ice-cube trays or pots and add frozen cubes to casseroles or sauces

what to make with gluts of fruit and vegetables

Even if you don't have a large vegetable patch, it's worth buying seasonal produce when it is at its cheapest and best and storing it for later months. Here's a list of ideas for ways to use various fruit and veg using recipes in the book (not including the baby purées in the final chapter).

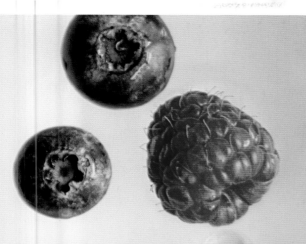

basics
and batches

apple sauce

1.25kg cooking apples, peeled and cored

This recipe is for a basic unsweetened purée, so it can be used in sweet and savoury dishes. I often mix the purée with a tin of apricots in natural juice and a sprinkle of sugar for a last-minute crumble filling. Or you can sweeten it a little and add it to softened onion, sage and a little cream for a delicious accompaniment to pork. Timings do vary depending on the microwave, so don't treat those I've given as gospel!

Makes 1 litre

Slice the apples fairly thinly and put into a saucepan or a dish suitable for the microwave. Add a dash of water then cook over a gentle heat, stirring occasionally, until the apples are soft. If you prefer, add a splash of water to the microwaveable dish (about 1cm in the bottom) and cover with a lid or cling film, pierced with one small steam hole. Microwave on high for 8 minutes. Stir the apples and return the dish to the microwave for 4 minutes, or until the apples are soft. Purée if you prefer a completely smooth texture, or leave slightly chunky.

(F) Cool, then transfer to bags or pots, label and freeze.

(D) Leave for about 3–4 hours at room temperature or defrost in the microwave ('Defrost' setting).

(R) Put in a pan over a low heat, or in a bowl in the microwave, until hot.

dark chocolate sauce

175ml whole milk
2 tablespoons cocoa powder
2 tablespoons golden syrup
50g butter, diced
150g bar good-quality dark chocolate,
    broken into pieces

Ice cream and chocolate sauce is the most comforting no-work pudding, and a favourite of my father-in-law, which makes his visits easy! Try it over poached pears or pancakes too, with a dollop of cream.

Makes 400ml

Put a little of the milk into a pan with the cocoa and mix to a paste. Add the remaining milk and golden syrup and heat until nearly boiling. Remove the pan from the heat, leave for a minute to cool slightly, then add the butter and chocolate and stir until melted.

(**F**) Pour the sauce into a container and cool, then cover, label and freeze.

(**D**) Put the container into a bowl of hot water and stir occasionally (will take about 30 minutes), or defrost at room temperature.

(**R**) Spoon the sauce into a heatproof bowl and reheat over a pan of simmering water, or microwave with care.

Variation:

Rum and chocolate sauce – Stir in 1–2 tablespoons of rum before freezing.

white chocolate sauce

300ml double cream
300g good-quality white chocolate
knob of butter

This is a great sauce to serve hot poured over frozen summer berries.

Makes 400ml

Put all the ingredients into a heatproof bowl placed over a pan of barely simmering water, and stir until the chocolate and butter have melted.

(**F**) Pour into a container, cool, then cover, label and freeze.

(**D**) Put the container into a bowl of hot water and stir occasionally (this will take about 30 minutes), or defrost at room temperature.

(**R**) Spoon the sauce into a heatproof bowl and reheat over a pan of simmering water, or microwave with care.

all-in-one white sauce

50g butter
50g plain flour
600ml milk

I've converted to this simple white sauce, purely because I'm always in a hurry and this is just as good as a traditionally made béchamel if it is to be used for a lasagne or cauliflower cheese. However, if, like my father, you prefer to make it the traditional way, then use the same quantities, but melt the butter, stir in the flour and gradually incorporate the milk. This makes a thickish sauce, so just add more milk if you like it runnier.

Makes 700ml

Put all the ingredients into a pan over a gentle heat and whisk continuously. The butter will gradually melt and the sauce will then thicken. Use a spoon to scrape around the edges of the pan or you risk the sauce being lumpy. Bring to the boil, then season and simmer for 2 minutes.

(F) Pour into a container, place some cling film over the surface of the sauce (to prevent a skin forming) and leave to cool, then remove the cling film, cover, label and freeze.

(D) Can be defrosted at room temperature (if not too warm) – leave for 4–6 hours.

Variations:

Cheese sauce – Stir 75g grated cheese into the sauce as it simmers.

Parsley sauce – Melt the butter first and add 3 tablespoons of chopped fresh parsley. Cook very gently for a minute or so then stir in the flour and gradually incorporate the milk. Season with salt and pepper, bring to the boil and simmer for 2 minutes.

Mushroom sauce – Sauté 6 sliced mushrooms in the butter, then add the flour and stir before gradually incorporating the milk. Season with salt and pepper, bring to the boil and simmer for 2 minutes.

Prawn sauce – Add a good handful of defrosted cooked and peeled prawns to the sauce once it has been defrosted and reheated. Simmer for 3–5 minutes or until piping hot. Do not refreeze.

bread sauce

700ml whole milk
1/2 onion
8 cloves
2 bay leaves
100g breadcrumbs
big knob of butter

Dead simple to make, this rich and creamy sauce is an absolute must with roast chicken.

Makes 750ml (enough for 6–8 servings)

Put the milk into a pan and begin to heat gently. Meanwhile, stud the onion with the cloves and then add to the pan along with the bay leaves and some salt and pepper. Continue to heat as gently as you can until the milk is hot but not boiling. Add the breadcrumbs, stir and leave for 20 minutes. Remove the onion and bay leaves and transfer the sauce to a container or two.

(F) Cool, then cover, label and freeze.

(D) Leave overnight in the fridge (or put in the microwave on 'defrost').

(R) Reheat gently in a pan, stirring in the butter just before serving.

breadcrumbs

8 slices (about 300g) ready-sliced,
    day-old soft-crusted bread

Have these at the ready to coat goujons of fresh chicken or fish, filling a treacle tart or queen of puddings or for use in the above!

Makes 300g

Break the bread into the bowl of a food processor and whizz until fine.

(F) Transfer to 2 small bags, putting 150g in each for ease. Label and freeze. There's generally no need to defrost before using.

madeira sauce

15g butter
1/2 large onion, finely chopped
1 level tablespoon plain flour
3 thyme sprigs
1 bay leaf
250ml beef consommé or beef stock
1 tablespoon redcurrant jelly
1 heaped teaspoon tomato ketchup
6 tablespoons Madeira

This is a great freezer standby as it is the perfect accompaniment to beef or lamb and is a great help when you are making something that doesn't have juices for gravy, such as the Beef Wellington on page 80. This is a much-simplified version of a favourite recipe that my mother used to make to go with rack of lamb.

Makes 250ml

Melt the butter in a pan over a gentle heat, add the onion and cook gently for 5–10 minutes to soften. Add the flour and stir, before adding the herbs, consommé or stock, redcurrant jelly, ketchup and salt and pepper. Simmer for 10 minutes, then add the Madeira and simmer for a further 5–10 minutes. Season to taste.

(F) Remove the herbs then cool before freezing.

(D) Leave at room temperature for about 4–6 hours.

(R) Warm gently in a pan.

chicken stock

2 roast chicken carcasses
2 celery sticks, chopped
1 large carrot, chopped
1 large onion, chopped
8 peppercorns
a few thyme sprigs
2 bay leaves
a small bunch of parsley,
   leaves and stalks
2.5 litres cold water

I have to say I've never once made chicken stock from raw bones, but I do find making stock from a roast chicken carcass a pretty easy pastime: you can simply throw it into a pot and let it bubble away while you read the Sunday papers. The end result is wonderful and a lot cheaper than buying a pot of fresh chicken stock. Remember, though, that you'll need to add extra salt if you're using this stock as a replacement for a cube.

Makes about 1.5 litres

Put everything into a large pan and bring slowly to the boil, then simmer for about 2 hours. Strain through a sieve into pots or bags.

(F) Leave to cool before labelling and freezing.

(D) Leave at room temperature for about 4–6 hours, depending on container size.

(R) Add to recipes as required.

sweet pastry

250g pack of butter, softened
125g caster sugar
1 whole large egg plus 1 egg yolk
500g plain flour, sifted
1 tablespoon cold water

Makes about 1kg

Cream the butter and sugar together in a food processor. Add the eggs and blend again. Add the flour and water, blend for a further 5 seconds, then scrape down the sides of the bowl and blend again until all the ingredients are just combined and forming a lump. Bring the pastry together using your hands and then weigh and divide it into portions of whatever size you like.

(F) Wrap tightly in a freezer bag and label then freeze.

(D) Leave at room temperature for about 1–2 hours, then use as needed.

shortcrust pastry

500g plain flour
125g butter, cold, cubed
125g lard, cold, cubed
a good pinch of salt
ice-cold water

Makes about 800g

Put the flour, fats and salt into a food processor. Pulse until crumb-like, then add water little by little until the mixture comes together. Bring the pastry together using your hands. Roll out onto a floured surface, fold up, then divide into portions of whatever size you like.

(F) Wrap tightly in a freezer bag and label then freeze.

(D) Leave at room temperature for about 1–2 hours, then use as needed.

yorkshire puddings

3 large eggs
approx 175ml plain flour
approx 175ml semi-skimmed milk or
   whole milk mixed with a little water
2 pinches of sea salt flakes
sunflower or vegetable oil,
   for cooking

This is the easiest recipe ever! If you have only two eggs then just measure their volume and use the same volume of flour and milk. Equally, you can double the batch and make more. If you remember when reheating them, a drizzle of beef roasting juices in the middle of the Yorkshires makes them even more flavoursome.

Makes 12–14

You will need a 12–15 cup muffin tin

Preheat the oven to 230°C/220°C fan/gas mark 8. Crack the eggs into the jug and measure their volume. Transfer to a bowl. Wash and dry the jug then measure exactly the same volume of flour and sieve into the bowl on top of the eggs. Pour the same volume of milk into the jug. Whisk the eggs and flour together with the salt flakes and a grind of black pepper. Gradually whisk in the milk. When the batter is smooth, pour it back into the jug.

Pour about half a teaspoon of oil into the bottom of each of the muffin cups. Place the tin in the oven to heat for 10 minutes. When the oil is scorchingly hot, pour the batter into each cup to about a third of the way up. Quickly put the tin back into the oven and cook for about 12–15 minutes, opening the door just at the end of the cooking time to check (they won't rise so well if you keep opening the door). Turn each pudding upside down in its cup and return the tin to the oven for a further couple of minutes to crisp up the bases, then remove and turn the Yorkshires onto a cooling rack to cool.

(**F**) Open freeze then transfer to a bag and label. You can also freeze the uncooked Yorkshire pudding mixture if you prefer (or have some left over), then defrost and cook as above.

(**R**) Cook from frozen for 5–10 minutes in a preheated hot oven (about 200°C/190°C fan/gas mark 6). The temperature doesn't have to be exact, so you can simply put them in the oven as you are finishing off your roast.

custard

I love custard in every form! The recipe below is idiot proof and won't curdle, I promise! This makes quite a runny custard; if you prefer yours thicker, then just add another teaspoon of cornflour.

Makes 400ml

250ml whole milk
100ml double cream
1 teaspoon best-quality vanilla extract with seeds or 1 pod, scraped and seeds added
2 large egg yolks
1 1/2 tablespoons golden caster sugar
1 heaped teaspoon cornflour

Pour the milk and cream into a pan and add the vanilla. Heat gently until hot but not boiling. Meanwhile, in a bowl, whisk the eggs yolks, sugar and cornflour. Whisk the hot milk and cream into the egg mixture to combine, then pour the mixture back into the pan and cook gently, stirring all the time, until the custard has thickened – about 3–4 minutes.

(**F**) Pour into a container, cover the surface with cling film while it cools (to prevent a skin forming). Remove the cling film, cover, label and freeze.

(**D**) Leave overnight in the fridge.

(**R**) Warm gently in a pan.

pancakes

Both the batter and the cooked pancakes are suitable for freezing.

Makes 6 pancakes

125g plain flour
1 large egg
1/2 teaspoon vegetable or sunflower oil
pinch of salt
300ml whole milk
about 25g butter

Put the flour, egg, oil, salt and half the milk into a bowl or blender and whisk or blend until smooth. Add the remaining milk and whisk or blend again.

Melt a little of the butter and use a pastry brush to distribute a small amount evenly all over a pancake pan or frying pan. Add a ladleful of the batter and tip the pan around until it is evenly covered with a thin layer of the mixture. Cook over a medium heat until beginning to brown. Use a palette knife to turn the pancake over (or flip it!). Cook the other side, then transfer to a sheet of greaseproof paper. Repeat with the remaining mixture, layering each pancake between sheets of greaseproof paper.

(**F**) Wrap the parcel of cooled layered pancakes in foil and freeze.

(**D**) Leave at room temperature for about 1–2 hours.

(**R**) Warm the parcel in a medium oven or in the microwave.

all-purpose tomato sauce

3 tablespoons olive oil
2 large red onions, peeled and finely chopped
2kg fresh very ripe tomatoes
3 garlic cloves, peeled and crushed
2 teaspoons caster sugar
1 1/2 tablespoons balsamic vinegar

I've nicknamed this 'glut of tomato sauce' as it used up all our home-grown tomatoes in one hit! I've kept the recipe simple and tasty, but it adapts well to the addition of some chilli, carrot, courgette or freshly chopped basil. Tweak it as you wish and use it in pasta sauces, as a base for Bolognese, a topping for Pizza (see page 160) or a sauce for Chicken with Chorizo, Peppers and Olives (see page 84). The options are endless!

Makes 1.3 litres

Heat the oil gently in a large pan, add the onions and soften them really gently over a low heat for about 15–20 minutes. Meanwhile, place the tomatoes in a large bowl and pour over boiling water to cover them. After a minute, drain off the water and slip off their skins (this really doesn't take long). Then roughly chop them, discarding any tough cores.

Add the garlic and sugar to the onions and fry for a further 5 minutes, stirring every so often. Add the tomatoes and their juices, balsamic vinegar and some salt and pepper to the pan, then cook gently for 1–1 1/2 hours, or until the tomato sauce has thickened, but is still of a pourable consistency.

(**F**) Cool, divide into freezer containers or bags, cover, label and freeze.

(**D**) Defrost at room temperature for about 4–5 hours, depending on quantity.

(**R**) Use in recipes or warm in a pan over a low heat, or microwave.

mince for all occasions

3–4 tablespoons olive oil
2kg good-quality beef mince
4 onions, peeled and chopped
6 large carrots, peeled and chopped
4 sticks celery, trimmed and sliced
4 garlic cloves, crushed
4 heaped teaspoons tomato purée
2 tablespoons plain flour
3 bay leaves
4 teaspoons Worcestershire sauce
2 x 400g tins chopped tomatoes
1 litre beef stock

This is a sort of combination of Bolognese sauce and cottage-pie filling. If you want to make the former, just add a squeeze of tomato purée and some mushrooms when reheating. If it's for cottage pie, simply reheat, adding some frozen peas if you like, and top with creamy root-veg mash. You can also use this to make the Beef and Spinach Lasagne on page 98.

Makes 12 portions

Put a tablespoon of the oil into a large frying pan and heat. Add about a third of the mince and, over a high heat, brown all over. Using a slotted spoon, remove it to a bowl, then fry the remaining mince in two batches, adding a little more oil as needed, removing to the bowl when browned.

Add the onions, carrots and celery to the pan. Fry gently, stirring every so often for about 10 minutes. Transfer the meat and vegetables to a large saucepan (or two if need be). Add the garlic, tomato purée and flour and stir over the heat for a further couple of minutes. Add the bay leaves, Worcestershire sauce, tomatoes and stock. Stir, season with salt and black pepper and simmer for 45 minutes, stirring every so often.

(F) Cool, then divide into quantities required, in lidded containers or bags, then label and freeze.

(D) Leave overnight in the fridge.

(R) Use in recipes or warm in a pan over a gentle heat.

chicken with white wine and herbs

8 chicken legs

3 bay leaves

1 teaspoon dried tarragon

15 peppercorns

30g (medium-sized bunch) fresh
    parsley, leaves and stalks separated

200ml dry white wine

4 celery sticks, trimmed

4 medium-sized onions, peeled and
    halved

6 medium carrots, peeled

knob of butter

350g chestnut mushrooms, quartered

2 garlic cloves, crushed

4 heaped tablespoons plain flour

a dash of soy sauce

3 tablespoons double cream

My brother, Al, is an inspiring teacher at Jamie Oliver's cooking school, Recipease. This is an adaptation of one of his favourite recipes to enjoy at home. For a wonderful spring stew try adding some blanched asparagus, peas and beans, or top it with pastry for a comforting pie (see page 86).

Serves 8

Put the chicken legs, bay leaves, tarragon, peppercorns, parsley stalks, white wine and 2 celery sticks into a large saucepan. Halve 2 of the onions and 2 of the carrots and add to the pan, then pour in enough cold water to cover the legs (about 2 litres). Cover the pan and bring to the boil, then reduce to a simmer and cook, with the lid half on, for 25 minutes, or until juices in the legs run clear.

Remove the chicken legs from the pan and set aside, but keep the stock simmering. Meanwhile, finely chop the remaining onion, carrot and celery into small chunks.

Heat the butter in a large pan over a low heat, add the chopped vegetables and a pinch of salt and sweat for 6–8 minutes. Meanwhile, strip the chicken from the bones and set aside. Put the bones, skin and trimmings back into the simmering stock pan and continue to simmer.

Put the mushrooms and garlic in the pan with the chopped vegetables and turn up the heat to brown all the ingredients (3–4 minutes). Stir in the flour and cook gently for a minute. Strain the stock into a jug and measure out 800ml (you can freeze any extra). Add nearly all of the stock and the soy sauce to the pan of vegetables, stirring it in slowly until it comes back to the simmer and thickens. Add a little more stock if it is still too thick – it should be thick enough to coat the back of a spoon. Chop the parsley leaves and add to the pan, along with the chicken. Stir in the cream, then taste and adjust seasoning as needed.

(**F**) Pour into containers of the size you require (if you are making the Chicken, Ham and Tarragon Pie on page 86 you will need to keep back about half). Allow to cool before covering, labelling and freezing.

(**D**) Leave overnight in the fridge.

(**R**) Place in a pan over a gentle heat until piping hot.

thai green curry paste

8 kaffir lime leaves, shredded

4 shallots, peeled and sliced

4 green chillies, deseeded and chopped into 1cm chunks

4 garlic cloves, peeled and chopped

2 lemongrass stalks, trimmed and finely chopped

1 x 5cm piece of ginger, peeled and chopped

75g bunch coriander, stalks and leaves

handful of basil leaves

1 1/2 teaspoons soft dark brown sugar or palm sugar

1 teaspoon sea salt flakes

1 teaspoon ground coriander

3/4 teaspoon Thai five-spice powder (optional)

2 tablespoons sunflower oil

2 tablespoons green peppercorns, drained

Whenever I had time, I always used to try and make my own Thai green curry paste instead of buying it in a jar. Now I just make a big batch and freeze it. It's infinitely better than shop bought, and using a whole big bunch of herbs and knob of ginger saves so much wastage. You can double this recipe if you want to make more. It's tricky to get the heat exactly right with chillies as they vary enormously. It's up to you to decide whether you want to make a hotter version by including the seeds. You can use this paste to make Coconut, Chicken and Butternut Squash Curry (page 66), Prawn and Noodle Broth (page 71) or Asian Beef Skewers (page 62).

Makes 15 smallish cubes (enough for about 10 portions of curry)

Put all the ingredients except the green peppercorns into a food processor with 2 tablespoons of water and whizz, scraping down the sides of the bowl every so often, until the mixture resembles a smooth paste. Transfer to a bowl and stir in the peppercorns.

(F) Spoon the sauce into an ice-cube tray and freeze. Then transfer the curry paste cubes from the tray into a bag, label and return to the freezer.

(R) Use 3 cubes for a 2-portion curry. Heat a little oil in a pan, add the frozen cubes and heat gently until defrosted, then stir-fry for a further 2 minutes before stirring in a can of coconut milk. Add your choice of chicken, prawns or vegetables, then, when cooked through, add a good dash of fish sauce and a squeeze of lime.

garlic bread

4 tablespoons softened butter

2 garlic cloves

1 tablespoon fresh parsley, chopped

1 large ciabatta or 400g pavé loaf (best quality you can find), cut 3/4 of the way down in 2.5cm-wide slices

It's rare that I buy garlic bread, and to be honest, unless you buy a 'taste-how-expensive-this-is' version, the baguettes are, I find, a bit disappointing. However, good homemade garlic bread is a real treat and delicious as a casual starter before a bowl of pasta with friends.

Serves 4–6

Mix the butter, garlic and parsley in a bowl and season with salt and pepper. Butter the insides of the slices of the loaf generously.

(F) Wrap the ciabatta or loaf in foil, place in a plastic bag and freeze.

(D) Remove from the freezer 2–3 hours before you need it.

(R) Preheat the oven to 220°C/200°C fan/gas mark 7. Place the foil parcel on a baking tray and bake for 15 minutes or until piping hot.

soups, starters and nibbles

spicy carrot, tomato, chorizo and coriander soup

1 tablespoon olive oil

1 red onion, finely chopped

1 x 250g pack cooking chorizo, deskinned and chopped (these look like sausages rather than salami)

400g carrots, cut into small chunks

400g sweet potatoes, peeled and cut into small chunks

3 celery sticks, cut into small chunks

1–2 teaspoons crushed dried chillies

1 teaspoon cumin seeds

1/2 teaspoon ground coriander

1/2 teaspoon turmeric

350g tomatoes, chopped

1 litre chicken stock

30g bunch coriander, chopped

1 x 400g tin chickpeas, drained

juice of 1 lime

To serve

wedges of bread and Manchego cheese (optional)

We have a small embarrassment in our house in that my husband has thus far produced nothing but knobbly carrots in his vegetable patch. We are told it's because we have stones in our soil, but as neither of us has the energy to rectify the problem by getting rid of the stones, I am stuck with misshapen, leggy carrots to cook with. This soupy stew is the answer and I feel happy that our rather ugly carrots now have the opportunity to shine!

Makes 1.7 litres

Heat the oil in a large pan and add the onion and chorizo. Fry gently for 5 minutes, before adding the carrots, sweet potato and celery. Continue to fry for a further 10 minutes, stirring occasionally. Add the spices and cook for 2 minutes, then add the tomatoes and stock. Season generously, bring to the boil and simmer for 20 minutes, or until the vegetables are tender.

Transfer about 4 ladlefuls of soup into a liquidizer and add half the coriander and chickpeas. Purée the soup until smooth then pour back into the pan with the remaining chickpeas, coriander and a good squeeze of lime. Stir together and taste for seasoning, adding more salt, pepper or lime as needed. Serve with wedges of bread and some Manchego cheese if you like.

(**F**) Pour into a container, cool, label and cover before freezing.

(**D**) Leave overnight in the fridge.

(**R**) Place in a pan over a low heat until hot.

creamy courgette, leek and parmesan soup

50g butter
2 medium leeks, trimmed and sliced
3 celery sticks, trimmed and finely chopped
1kg courgettes, thickly sliced
1 large garlic clove, chopped
2 rosemary sprigs
850ml well-flavoured chicken stock
75g Parmesan, grated
40g mature Cheddar, grated
300ml whole milk

To serve
2 tablespoons fresh parsley, chopped

The great thing about this soup is that as long as you also include some normal-sized courgettes, you can get rid of the whopping marrow-sized ones that you are bound to grow at least one of each season! Remove the tough seedy centres and peel of any large courgettes before weighing – I use yellow courgettes, which tend to have softer skins that are fine to cook.

Serves 6

Melt the butter in a large pan and fry the leeks and celery for 5 minutes. Add the courgettes and continue to fry for 10 minutes. Add the garlic and rosemary and stir over the heat for a further 3–4 minutes. Pour in the stock, season, cover with a lid and simmer for about 15 minutes, or until the vegetables are tender.

Remove the rosemary stalks, stir in the cheeses and then the milk. Purée the soup and taste for seasoning. Serve scattered with the parsley.

(F) Pour into a container, cool, label and cover before freezing.

(D) Leave overnight in the fridge.

(R) Place in a pan over a low heat until hot.

watercress and pea soup

25g butter
1 large onion, peeled and sliced
2 sticks celery, trimmed and sliced
250g potatoes, peeled and chopped
   into 5cm cubes
550ml chicken or vegetable stock
200g fresh or frozen peas
2 x 75g bags watercress
500ml whole milk

To serve
croutons and watercress sprigs
   (optional)

Living just next to the Hampshire watercress beds, I feel it's my duty to include at least one or two recipes that use this wonderfully nutritious leaf.

Makes 1.5 litres

Melt the butter in large pan, add the onion and fry gently for 6–8 minutes. Add the celery and potato and continue to fry for 5 minutes, stirring occasionally. Add the stock, bring to the boil, then simmer for 15 minutes or until the potato is tender.

Add the peas and watercress (reserving a few sprigs as garnish) and bring to a simmer, stirring to wilt the watercress, and simmer for a couple of minutes. Turn off the heat, stir in the milk, then purée the soup in a liquidiser or using a stick blender.

(**F**) Pour into a container, cool, cover, label and freeze.

(**D**) Leave overnight in the fridge.

(**R**) Pour into a pan and reheat gently. Ladle into bowls and serve garnished with watercress sprigs and crunchy croutons.

gazpacho

1/2 large cucumber, roughly chopped
1 green pepper, deseeded and cut
    into chunks
3 ripe vine tomatoes, cored and cut
    into wedges
1/2 small red onion, chopped
2 thick slices day-old white bread,
    torn into pieces
2 cloves garlic, chopped
2 1/2 tablespoons olive oil
2 1/2 tablespoons good-quality
    red wine or cider vinegar
pinch of sugar
400ml tomato juice
Tabasco, to taste (optional)

This is great served really cold in shot glasses on a warm summer's evening. Alternatively, serve it in bowls with some cooked and peeled prawns, drizzled with lemon and oil, or with some chopped blanched almonds sprinkled on top.

Makes 1 litre

Put the cucumber, pepper, tomatoes, onion, bread, garlic, oil, vinegar and sugar into a bowl with some salt and pepper and stir together. Leave for 4 hours or overnight for the flavours to infuse. Blend in a liquidiser until completely smooth, then add the tomato juice and taste for seasoning, adding a splash of Tabasco if you like.

(F) Pour into a container, cover, label and freeze.

(D) Leave overnight in the fridge.

velvety butternut squash soup

50g butter
1 large onion, peeled and chopped
1kg butternut squash, peeled,
 deseeded and cut into chunks
2 large carrots, peeled and cut
 into chunks
350ml good-strength chicken stock
700ml whole milk
pinch of grated nutmeg

I'm fully aware that there are a million butternut squash soups out there, but I still think this one, with the addition of carrot, beats them all! Use a liquidiser rather than a stick blender for an even smoother soup.

Makes 1.8 litres

Melt the butter, add the onion and soften gently for 5–8 minutes while you prepare the other vegetables. Add the butternut squash and carrot and continue to cook gently for about 10 minutes, stirring every so often. Pour the stock and milk into the pan, bring to a simmer, but do not boil. Leave to simmer for about 20 minutes, then season generously with salt, pepper and nutmeg, before whizzing in a liquidiser and tasting for further seasoning.

(**F**) Pour into a container, cool, label and cover before freezing.

(**D**) Leave overnight in the fridge.

(**R**) Put into a pan and reheat gently.

haddock chowder

25g butter
2 teaspoons olive oil
1 large onion, chopped
4 medium potatoes (each weighing
   about 175g), unpeeled if new,
   and chopped into 2–3cm cubes
1 tablespoon thyme leaves
splash of white wine
500ml good-strength chicken stock
750ml whole milk
2 x 198g tins sweetcorn drained,
   or 2 large corn on the cobs,
   niblets removed
450g undyed smoked haddock fillet,
   cut into 4cm chunks

To serve
5 slices streaky bacon, chopped
2 tablespoons double cream
handful of chives, snipped

Chowders are by far my favourite kinds of soup and often feature at our table on a Saturday lunchtime. The best, I think is clam, followed closely by haddock. If you can, try and buy some really good-quality Scottish smoked undyed haddock, which has a more subtle flavour than some of the others.

Serves 4

Heat the butter and oil and add the onion. Cook over a low heat for 5 minutes, then add the potatoes and cook for a further 5 minutes. Add the thyme and wine and boil for a minute or so before pouring in the stock and stirring. Add the milk and bring to nearly boiling, then reduce the heat and simmer for 10 minutes or so until the potatoes are nearly tender.

Add the sweetcorn, haddock and a grind of pepper and bring to a simmer. Cook for a further 10 minutes, or until the haddock is just cooked. Taste for seasoning, adding a little salt if needed.

(F) Pour into a container, cool, label and cover before freezing.

(D) Leave overnight in the fridge.

(R) Pour into a pan and gently reheat, trying not to break up the fish.

(S) Heat a frying pan and add the bacon. Cook until crisp, then drain on kitchen paper. Ladle the soup into bowls and top each with a swirl of cream, some crispy bacon and a sprinkle of chives.

sausage rolls with mustard and poppy seeds

1 x 400g pack good-quality herby
   sausages
plain flour, for dusting
500g homemade Shortcrust Pastry
   (see page 28) or 500g pack all-butter
   shortcrust pastry, defrosted
1 egg, beaten
2–3 tablespoons English or Dijon
   mustard, onion marmalade or some
   chilli jam if you prefer
poppy (or sesame) seeds,
   for sprinkling

My mother has been making lovely crescent-shaped sausage rolls for years. She can't remember which party book she originally found the recipe in, and I have changed it somewhat, but a big thank you to whoever came up with the idea of rolling them like a croissant! Don't scrimp on sausage meat inside or you will end up with a mouthful of pastry! You can also use flavoured sausage meat, if you prefer.

Makes 18

Preheat the oven to 200°C/180°C fan/gas mark 6.

Split the sausages using a sharp knife, then squeeze the sausage meat from the skins into a bowl. Divide into about 18 equal-sized pieces. Roll each piece into a baby chipolata shape (long and thin rather than dumpy!)

On a generously floured surface, roll out the pastry thinly and trim the edges so that you have a square of about 33cm x 33cm. Cut the pastry lengthways into 3 equal strips and cut each strip into three squares. Then cut each square in half diagonally so that you have 18 triangles.

Brush the edges of a pastry triangle with egg, then place a small dollop of mustard, onion marmalade or chilli jam and some sausage meat in the middle. Roll the triangle up tightly towards the point, folding round the outer edges to seal. (Don't worry if you can still see a little of the sausage peeking through.) Brush all over with more egg and sprinkle with poppy or sesame seeds. Repeat with the remaining triangles. Place all the sausage rolls on a baking tray lined with greaseproof or waxed paper and bake for 20–25 minutes.

(F) Cool, then freeze between sheets of greaseproof or waxed paper in a box, or open freeze then place in a bag.

(R) Cook from frozen in a preheated oven at 200°C/180°C fan/gas mark 6 for about 8 minutes, or until piping hot.

two easy freezer pâtés

If I was organised enough, I'd always have a stash of these pâtés in the freezer. Rather like potted shrimps, another favourite, these little dishes are really useful for a Saturday lunch or a casual supper with friends.

Smoked trout pâté

Serves 4–6

150g butter
1 x 125g pack hot-smoked trout fillets
1 x 100g pack smoked trout
zest and juice of 1/2 large lemon
5 tablespoons double cream
1 teaspoon anchovy sauce or 2 anchovy
   fillets in oil, drained and chopped

To serve
hot toast and lemon wedges

Melt the butter in a pan over a low heat or in the microwave, then cool for about 5 minutes. Meanwhile, put the hot-smoked trout fillets and half the smoked trout in a food-processor. Add the lemon juice and zest, cream, anchovy sauce or chopped anchovy fillets and a good grinding of black pepper. Pour in 3/4 of the melted butter. Process, scraping down the sides of the bowl once, until smooth. Tear up the remaining half pack of smoked trout and add to the food-processor. Pulse until it is mixed in but the pâté is still a bit textured. Taste for seasoning, then divide between 4–6 pots (or spoon into one larger dish) and cover with the remaining butter. Chill.

Chicken liver parfait

Serves 6–8

250g butter
1 teaspoon vegetable oil
400g fresh chicken livers, roughly
   chopped if large
1/2 small onion, chopped
1 teaspoon thyme leaves
2 parsley stalks
1 bay leaf
good splash of brandy, Madeira or
   sweet sherry

To serve
hot toast, onion marmalade or chutney
   and a squeeze of lemon

Put 75g of the butter into a pan (or the microwave in a bowl) over a low heat and melt it very gently. Set aside. Melt 75g of the remaining butter in a frying pan with the oil. Add the onion and soften, then turn up the heat, add the chicken livers, herbs and a good seasoning of salt and pepper and stir-fry for 3–4 minutes. Add the brandy (or Madeira or sherry) and continue to cook for 2 minutes. Remove from the heat and cool slightly, then remove the bay leaf and any herb stalks and blitz the chicken livers in a blender until smooth. Dice the remaining butter and add to the blender with the motor still running. Taste and adjust seasoning if necessary.

If you want a very smooth pâté, pass the mixture through a sieve into a bowl. Spoon the pâté into individual pots or one large dish. Smooth the tops and gently pour the reserved melted butter over the top to cover. Chill.

(F) Cover the pots, then label and freeze.

(D) Leave overnight in the fridge.

(S) Remove from the fridge up to an hour before serving so that it softens a little.

game terrine with pink peppercorns

4 tablespoons brandy

14 ready-to-eat pitted prunes

2 rabbits, boned (total boned weight approximately 800g)

750g pork belly slices, de-rinded and chopped into 1–2cm chunks

knob of butter

splash of vegetable oil

1 small onion, chopped

2 rabbit livers

2 garlic cloves, chopped

1/2 x 206g pack cubetti di pancetta

1/2 teaspoon ground allspice

1/2 teaspoon thyme leaves

2 eggs, beaten

6 tablespoons good quality chicken stock

2 level teaspoons sea salt flakes

2 teaspoons pink peppercorns in brine, drained

1 x 300g pack, or about 12 slices, smoked streaky bacon

To serve

hot toast, rocket salad and cornichons

If you aren't a fan of rabbit, pheasant or chicken also work well.

Makes 2 x 900g loaves, each serving 8–10

You will need 2 x 900g loaf tins.

Put half the brandy and all the prunes into a small bowl and leave to soak. Preheat the oven to 180°C/160°C fan/gas mark 4.

Set aside about half of the boned rabbit to use in the middle of the terrine. Choose the loin fillets for this, plus a little extra of the remaining meat if needed, and cut into long fairly thick strips. Cut the remaining meat into smallish pieces and put into a bowl with the chopped pork belly.

Melt the butter and oil in a frying pan and fry the onion until softened – about 5–8 minutes. Add the livers and garlic and stir-fry until sealed. Add the remaining brandy and cook for a further couple of minutes, then transfer to the bowl of pork and rabbit, along with the cubetti di pancetta, allspice, thyme, eggs, stock, salt and a good grinding of pepper. Stir together then transfer to a food-processor in batches (depending on the size and strength of your machine) and blitz until it has a chunky mince-like texture – it should not be smooth. Transfer back to the bowl and stir in the pink peppercorns.

Line the 2 loaf tins with the bacon rashers, laying them side by side across the tin, with their ends hanging over the sides. Spoon half the mixture into the tins and lay the prunes in a line lengthways down the middle. Put the whole pieces of rabbit next to the prunes, filling all the remaining space, then top with the remaining mixture and lay the bacon ends over the top. Wrap each tin completely in foil then sit them in a roasting tin. Fill 3/4 of the way up with boiling water, then bake the terrines for 1 1/2 hours.

Remove from the oven and cool, then wrap the loaf tins in cling film, place weights on top (tins or scales weights would be perfect for this) and refrigerate overnight.

(F) Remove the terrines from their tins, clean off any jelly from the outside, wrap in cling film and foil and freeze.

(D) Leave overnight in the fridge.

(S) Remove from the fridge up to an hour before serving. Slice the terrines and serve with hot toast, rocket salad and cornichons.

courgette and sweetcorn cakes with smoked salmon

200g plain flour
1 tablespoon baking powder
2 large eggs, beaten
1 heaped teaspoon sea salt flakes
3 pinches cayenne pepper
1 1/2 tablespoons snipped chives
175ml whole milk
25g butter, melted, plus knob of butter
    for frying
175g courgette, trimmed and grated
2 x 100g corn on the cobs, cooked and
    niblets removed, or 150g tinned
    sweetcorn, drained

To serve
200g pack smoked salmon
8 tablespoons crème fraîche
1/2 small red onion, very thinly sliced
baby capers, snipped chives and lemon
    wedges

These were on the menu at a restaurant where I worked in Port Douglas, Australia. They also make a delicious alternative to blinis if you make them canapé sized.

Makes 8 pancakes (1 per person as a starter)

Put the flour, baking powder, eggs, salt, cayenne pepper and chives into a bowl. Add the milk, melted butter and a good grind of pepper and beat with a whisk. Add the courgette and corn niblets and stir.

Melt a knob of butter in a large frying pan and spoon in the pancake mixture in dollops (about 1 1/2 tablespoons per pancake) to make 3 pancakes in the pan (they should be quite thick). Leave them to cook gently for five minutes or so, then turn them over when golden and cook the other sides.

(F) Transfer the cakes to greaseproof paper sheets and freeze.

(D) Place on a baking tray and leave for 2 hours at room temperature.

(R) Preheat the oven to 160°C/150°C fan/gas mark 3. Put the baking tray into the oven for 10–15 minutes or until the cakes are hot.

(S) Place the cakes onto plates and top each with a mound of smoked salmon, a good dollop of crème fraîche, some thinly sliced red onion, capers and snipped chives. Serve with lemon wedges.

leek and stilton tarts

400g homemade Shortcrust Pastry
(see page 28) or 1 x 375g pack ready-
rolled shortcrust pastry sheets
25g butter
3 medium leeks, trimmed and finely
chopped
2 eggs and 1 egg yolk
250ml double cream
150g Stilton cheese, crumbled

To serve
dressed salad leaves

These are starter sized, but feel free to make them smaller or larger if you like. There are lots of other versions you can make with the same egg mix poured over – bacon and pea, caramelised onion or broccoli to give you just a few ideas.

Makes 6

You will need 6 small loose-bottomed tartlet cases of about 11–12.5cm diameter at the base and baking beans.

On a floured surface, roll out the pastry until really thin. (Even ready-rolled pastry benefits from being a little bit thinner as you then get a crisp base and a better filling to pastry ratio). Cut out rounds from the pastry to line your tartlet cases and prick the bases. Cut circles of greaseproof paper large enough to line each case. Scrunch up these paper cases then open them up again, place inside the tartlet cases and fill with baking beans. Place the tartlet cases on a baking sheet and bake for 5 minutes, before removing the beans and paper and drying out in the oven for a further 5 minutes or so.

Meanwhile, heat the butter in a pan and fry the leeks very gently until softened (about 10 minutes), stirring every so often. In a bowl, beat the eggs and the cream with some seasoning.

Remove the tartlets from the oven and divide the leeks between each one, then top with the crumbled Stilton. Finally pour in the egg mix until it reaches the top of each case. Bake for approximately 15–20 minutes or until risen and golden. Remove from the oven and cool.

(F) When cool, remove the tartlets from the tins and open freeze. Then wrap in foil or place in a container, cover and label.

(R) Place the frozen tartlets on a baking tray and bake at 180°C/160°C fan/ gas mark 4 for 15–20 minutes or until piping hot. (Cover with foil if necessary to prevent them becoming too brown.)

This also works in a larger 24cm diameter x 2.5cm depth quiche tin. Cook for 30 minutes and reheat from frozen covered with foil at 180°C/160°C fan/ gas mark 4 for 45–55 minutes, or until piping hot.

tamarind and prawn parcels

2 teaspoons oil
1 onion, finely chopped
1 garlic clove, crushed
2.5cm knob of ginger, peeled and
  chopped
1/2 large red chilli, deseeded and
  chopped
14 cherry tomatoes, halved
2 tablespoons tamarind pulp
juice of 1/2 lime
1 1/2 teaspoons fish sauce
2 tablespoons chopped fresh coriander
220g raw peeled tiger prawns (make
  sure that they have not been
  previously frozen), chopped into
  1 1/2 cm chunks
1 x 270g pack filo pastry (6 sheets),
  defrosted
75g butter, melted, plus 50g more for
  brushing once defrosted

To serve
salad leaves and mango chutney

Make these as a starter, or smaller versions for canapés. They are delicious served warm from the oven with a few leaves on the side and maybe some mango chutney for dipping. Keep the seeds in the chilli if you want a more fiery end result.

Makes 12 parcels (serves 6 as a starter)

Heat the oil in a pan and gently fry the onion until softened (about 10 minutes). Add the garlic, ginger and chilli and continue to cook for 2–3 minutes. Then add the tomatoes, tamarind and lime and cook for 10 minutes, or until the tomatoes are soft. Stir in the fish sauce and remove the pan from the heat and allow to cool.

When completely cool, stir in the prawns and coriander.

Lay the sheets of filo out on a clean surface and cover with a damp tea towel. Take one filo sheet and brush all over with the melted butter. Taking hold of one long side, fold it towards the middle. Brush again with the melted butter and fold in the other side to make a long triple-layered strip. Cut this in half so that you have two pieces approximately 20cm long and 8cm wide.

Place 2 teaspoons of the filling mixture at one end of the strip, leaving a 2cm border. Take the right corner and fold diagonally to the left, enclosing the filling and forming a triangle. Fold again along the upper crease of the triangle. Keep folding in this way until you reach the end of the strip. Place the parcel onto a tray covered in greaseproof paper. Continue until you have made all 12 parcels.

(F) Open freeze the unbaked parcels then transfer to a container, label and cover.

(C) Brush the frozen parcels with melted butter then bake at 200°C/180°C fan/gas mark 6 for 25 minutes or until golden. Serve with salad leaves and mango chutney (loosen with a little hot water).

700g good-quality sirloin steak, sliced into 7cm strips
vegetable oil, for brushing

For the spicy marinade
2.5cm piece of fresh ginger, peeled and finely chopped
1 large garlic clove, finely chopped
1 red chilli, deseeded and finely chopped
1 lemongrass stalk, very finely chopped
2 tablespoons soy
1 1/2 tablespoons fish sauce
2 teaspoons sesame oil

To serve
Asian-style salad made from cucumber ribbons, sliced spring onions and coriander leaves.
sweet chilli or satay sauce, for dipping

asian beef skewers

This recipe also works marinated with the Thai Green Curry Paste (see page 37) mixed with a little coconut milk. These are great for the barbecue, too.

Makes 12 skewers (serves 6 as a starter)

You will need 12 wooden or metal skewers.

Place all the marinade ingredients in a bowl and stir together. Add the steak and mix well. Cover the bowl and place in the fridge to marinate for 1 hour. Remove the meat strips from the marinade and thread onto skewers.

(F) Lay a freezer bag onto a plate and put the kebabs inside, lying them side by side. Freeze, then remove the plate from underneath and tie the bag.

(D) Leave to defrost thoroughly overnight.

(R) When ready to cook, heat a large griddle until smoking hot. Brush the kebabs with a little vegetable oil, then griddle the skewers, turning occasionally and pushing down on them with a fish slice, for a total of about 4–5 minutes. (Check, as griddles vary a lot.) Serve with the Asian-style salad and sweet chilli or satay sauce for dipping.

For the kebab
500g minced lamb
1 teaspoon ground cumin
1/2 teaspoon ground coriander
3/4 teaspoon hot chilli powder
1/2 teaspoon dried oregano
1 teaspoon fresh thyme leaves

To serve
6 flatbreads
250ml natural yogurt
1/2 cucumber, halved lengthways, deseeded and grated
1 small garlic clove, crushed
seeds of 1 pomegranate
1/2 red onion, finely sliced
handful of fresh mint leaves, chopped
lime wedges

spicy lamb kebabs

You can cook the kebabs on the barbecue if you like.

Serves 6

In a bowl, combine the kebab ingredients with 1 teaspoon sea salt and a good grinding of black pepper. Mix well until thoroughly combined. Divide into six equal portions and form each into a sausage shape around a kebab stick.

(F) Put the kebabs into a freezer bag, lying them side by side. Freeze on a plate, then remove the plate from underneath and tie the bag.

(D) Place in the fridge for 4–5 hours.

(S) Grill the kebabs for 10 minutes, turning, until cooked through and browned. Meanwhile, warm the flatbreads. Mix the yogurt with the cucumber, garlic and some salt and pepper. Serve the kebabs with the warmed flatbreads, the cucumber and yogurt sauce, red onion, mint leaves, pomegranate seeds and lime wedges.

suppers from the freezer

There are many bags of meat, poultry and seafood available in supermarkets that specify 'can be cooked from frozen', and with our 'no time but want to cook' attitude to preparing meals nowadays, they are exactly what we need. They are perfectly easy and safe to use, and there are no extras added – they have just been blast frozen as individual pieces and you simply cook them a little longer than you would fresh. Fingers crossed there are more to come – particularly good-quality free-range meat and poultry.

If you prefer, of course, you can freeze your own meat in easily removable packaging – burgers, sausages and chops are just some of the things that can be cooked from frozen – and I have found that the plus side to buying and freezing your own meat is that you can choose the best quality. Freeze items individually – flat, or side by side, rather than in a lump – otherwise you will find it tricky to ensure that they cook evenly and, most importantly, the whole way through. Wrap them tightly and you'll avoid freezer burn. Even better, ask your friendly butcher to pack your meat in sizes you require then vacuum pack it.

The recipes in this chapter all use meat or seafood that can be cooked from frozen, but you can also make them using fresh meat or seafood – just reduce the cooking time a little. All these dishes are also suitable for freezing once cooked. Just make sure that you defrost them in the fridge overnight and reheat until piping hot.

coconut, chicken and butternut squash curry

1 tablespoon sesame oil
3 cubes frozen Thai Green Curry
   Paste (see page 37), or 2 tablespoons
   from a jar
1/2 teaspoon ground coriander
1/2 teaspoon turmeric
400g frozen chicken chunks
   (or fresh chicken if you prefer)
400ml tin coconut milk
300g frozen or fresh butternut
   squash chunks
2 ripe tomatoes, chopped, or a
   handful of cherry tomatoes
1 x 250g tin bamboo shoots, drained
   and rinsed (optional)
2 tablespoons fish sauce
good squeeze of lime or lemon juice

To serve
basmati rice
1 tablespoon fresh coriander,
   chopped (optional)

The ultimate modern, quick meal – and yes, you really can add frozen chicken and butternut to this! Just make sure you buy chicken that has been frozen in similar-sized individual chunks, as this will ensure even cooking. You can use raw frozen prawns instead of chicken if you prefer. If you have any left over, you can freeze, defrost and reheat at another time.

Serves 2–3

Heat the sesame oil in a pan, add the curry paste and gently fry until defrosted (or add the shop-bought paste to the pan and fry for a minute). Add the ground coriander and turmeric and cook over a medium heat for 1–2 minutes. Add the frozen chicken chunks and half the can of coconut milk and bring to the boil, then lower the heat and simmer for 10 minutes.

Add the butternut squash, tomatoes and the rest of the coconut milk and bring back up to the boil. Reduce the heat to a simmer and continue cooking for a further 10–15 minutes, or until the squash is tender and chicken cooked through and piping hot. If using, add the bamboo shoots for the final 5 minutes of cooking time. Stir in the fish sauce and lime or lemon juice, to taste. Serve with basmati rice, garnished with chopped coriander, if using.

portuguese seafood stew

1 tablespoon olive oil

1 red onion, cut into wedges, or 3
handfuls of chopped frozen onion

2 peppers, deseeded and cut into
chunks (or frozen pepper slices –
add with the passata)

400g new potatoes, cut into smallish
chunks

1–2 pinches of crushed dried chillies

2 bay leaves

splash of white wine

1/2 x 680g jar of passata with garlic
and onions

1/2 pint chicken or vegetable stock

400g bag frozen mixed seafood (raw
squid, prawns, mussels and scallops),
or 400g fresh mixed seafood

handful of chopped fresh parsley
(optional)

To serve
garlic bread or salad

**Based on traditional Cataplana, this recipe uses a bag of cook-from-frozen
seafood, so makes a great supper standby. Serve it with garlic bread or
a big salad.**

Serves 4

Heat the olive oil in a wok or large pan, add the onions and peppers and sauté
for 5 minutes over a medium heat. Add the potatoes and fry for a further
7 minutes. Stir in the chillies, bay leaves and wine, then add the passata and
stock, stir and bring to the boil. Reduce the heat and simmer for 15 minutes.

Add the frozen seafood and cook for 8–10 minutes, or until the potatoes
are tender and the seafood cooked through and piping hot. Add the parsley
(if using) and serve.

fish pie pots

1 x 375g pack ready-rolled puff pastry

milk, for brushing

2 eggs

knob of butter

splash of oil

1 onion, finely chopped, or 3 good
   handfuls of frozen chopped onions

6 mushrooms, quartered

2 x 350g pots cheese sauce, or 1
   quantity Cheese Sauce (see page 22)

1¹/2 teaspoons Dijon mustard

2 x 400g packs frozen fish pie mix, or
   800g smoked and non-smoked fresh
   fish fillets, cut into chunks

200g frozen raw king prawns

2 teaspoons baby capers (optional)

2 heaped tablespoons parsley, chopped

I love those individual one-pot pies you often see, but, I don't know about you, I never have enough suitable ovenproof bowls or dishes to serve them in. So for this I've cheated! Choose any pretty bowls or dishes, as long as they can be warmed. If using frozen, take the pastry and cheese sauce out of the freezer in the morning, but you can cook the fish and prawns direct from frozen and you'll be able to create a smart fish pie with barely the flick of a wooden spoon! If you can't find the pre-frozen fish pie mix, buy separate bags of frozen prawns and fish and measure out what you need.

Serves 4–6, depending on the size of your dishes

Preheat the oven to 220°C/200°C fan/gas mark 7. Unroll the pastry and cut 4–6 discs or interesting shapes to sit on top of your bowls. Grease a baking tray or cut a rectangle of greaseproof paper to line your tray. Transfer the shapes to your tray and score each with a criss-cross pattern. Brush with milk and bake for 12–15 minutes, then remove and keep warm.

Meanwhile, boil the eggs for 6–8 minutes and make the sauce. Heat the butter and oil in a pan until the butter has melted, then add the onion and soften over a low heat for 3–4 minutes. Add the mushrooms and continue to fry for another 2–3 minutes. Add the cheese sauce, mustard and some ground black pepper and bring to a simmer. Stir in the frozen fish and prawns and gently simmer for about 10 minutes, stirring carefully every so often.

Drain the eggs, rinse in cold water, then peel and cut into pieces. Add to the fish, along with the capers (if using) and parsley. When the fish is cooked and piping hot, divide it between the dishes and top each with a pastry shape.

prawn and noodle broth

2 tablespoons flavourless oil, such as
   groundnut or sunflower
2 cubes frozen Thai Green Curry
   Paste (see page 37), or 1 rounded
   tablespoon from a jar
5 closed-cup or shiitake mushrooms,
   quartered (or 2 handfuls frozen
   mushroom slices)
400ml good-quality chicken stock
150g raw frozen prawns (look for a bag
   that says 'cook from frozen')
2 handfuls of stir-fry vegetables, such
   as babycorn, mangetout, pepper or
   frozen stir-fry vegetable mix
1 tablespoon fish sauce
juice of 1 lime
175g ready-cooked rice noodles
2 spring onions, sliced

Nothing beats this soup when you are on a bit of a health kick, or just fancy something light. Fragrant and full of crunchy vegetables, it's a real pick-me-up. Buy dried noodles and cook according to the pack instructions if you prefer.

Serves 2

Heat the oil in a pan, add the curry paste and gently fry until defrosted (or add the shop-bought paste to the pan and fry for a minute). Add the mushrooms and fry for 2 minutes. Add the chicken stock and heat until simmering, then stir in the prawns. Once the broth has come back to the boil, throw in the mixed vegetables. Cook for a further 3–5 minutes, or until the prawns are cooked through and piping hot. Stir in the fish sauce and lime juice.

Reheat the noodles following the pack instructions and divide between two bowls. Ladle on the soup and garnish with the spring onions .

pork chops with mustard, apples and cider

1 tablespoon olive oil

2 knobs of butter

4 x 200g bone-in thick pork chops, frozen (or fresh, if you prefer)

1 small onion, chopped, or 2 handfuls of frozen chopped onion

250g frozen cooking apple slices or 250g peeled and sliced fresh cooking apple

2 garlic cloves, chopped

8 sage leaves

250ml dry cider

1 1/2 heaped tablespoons grainy mustard

250ml chicken stock

2 tablespoons double cream (optional)

To serve

jacket potatoes

Using frozen chops in a braised dish like this one is no different from using fresh, as you are tenderising the pork in the cider and apple sauce, so the chops have no chance of drying out. Just make sure the chops are not frozen in a lump. If you have any left over, you can freeze, defrost and reheat on another occasion.

Serves 4

Preheat the oven to 160°C/150°C fan/gas mark 3. Heat the oil and a knob of butter in a frying pan and fry the frozen pork chops over a high heat until browned (about 5 minutes on each side). Season and transfer to a casserole.

Add a second knob of butter to the frying pan and, once melted, add the onions and stir-fry for 5 minutes. Add the apple slices, garlic and sage and stir-fry for a further 2–3 minutes, then transfer to the casserole.

Add the cider to the frying pan and bring to the boil, scraping the base of the pan to incorporate all the lovely flavours. Add the mustard and stir together, then pour over the pork and apples, along with the stock. Cover with a lid and bake in the oven for 1 1/2 hours.

Remove the pork chops to a baking dish and keep warm. Place the casserole over a medium heat and allow the gravy to bubble for 5 minutes or so to reduce and concentrate it a little. Stir in the double cream, if using, season to taste and serve with the chops and some jacket potatoes.

asparagus and pea risotto

knob of butter, plus 25g to stir in at
the end
2 teaspoons olive oil
1/2 onion, peeled and chopped, or 2
handfuls frozen chopped onions
4 mushrooms, quartered, or a large
handful frozen mushroom slices
1 garlic clove
200g carnaroli rice (or other risotto
rice, e.g. arborio)
splash of white wine (optional)
600–750ml hot vegetable stock
100g frozen peas
150g frozen or fresh asparagus spears,
snapped in half
2 tablespoons grated Parmesan cheese

Risotto is such a brilliant midweek standby, as you can adapt it to suit the contents of your fridge (or freezer) and this one is very colourful as well as being healthy too. Add chicken or prawns to this for a non-veggie version. You can also use some frozen baby broad beans if you are not in possession of any asparagus, or use fresh if in season.

Serves 2–3

Heat the knob of butter and oil in a deep frying or sauté pan and add the onion. Stir-fry gently for 3–4 minutes, then add the mushrooms and garlic and stir-fry for another minute or two. Add the rice and stir for a further 2 minutes, then pour in the wine, if using, or a ladleful of stock and stir until absorbed. Keep adding the stock, about 150–200ml at a time, letting it bubble and stirring every so often until it is absorbed by the rice.

When you have only about 200ml of stock left to add, test the rice. If it still has a crunch to it, add a bit more stock and cook gently for a little longer. Add the peas and asparagus with the final addition of stock. Allow the vegetables to cook for a couple of minutes, then remove the pan from the heat. The risotto should be creamy and silky, neither too soupy nor too dry (add a little more stock if necessary). Season, then stir in the grated Parmesan and the butter. Leave the risotto to rest for 5 minutes before ladling it into bowls.

sausages baked with puy lentils

12 frozen or fresh sausages
2 red peppers, deseeded, thickly sliced,
or 2 handfuls frozen pepper slices
2 red onions, peeled, cut into wedges
2 tablespoons olive oil
1 litre hot beef stock
1 tablespoon Dijon mustard

Buy really good-quality butchers sausages for this dish, not the bagged frozen ones – venison ones work really well, as do some of the more spicy varieties now available. Either ask your butcher to pack them side by side on a tray or just open freeze the individual sausages and take them out as you need them. If you've got defrosted ones to hand, simply reduce the browning time at the beginning.

Serves 4–6

1 teaspoon English mustard powder

1½ tablespoons tomato purée

2 garlic cloves, crushed

200g puy lentils

2 rosemary sprigs

2 bay leaves

Preheat the oven to 180°C/160°C fan/gas mark 4.

Put the sausages into a medium-sized roasting tin and bake for 35 minutes or until lightly browned (if cooking from fresh they will take a little less time). Remove the tin from the oven and add the peppers, red onion and oil. Toss together, then return to the oven for a further 10 minutes.

In a jug, mix the hot stock with the mustards, tomato purée, garlic and a good grinding of black pepper. Scatter the puy lentils over the sausages, then add the herbs and pour over the stock mixture. Stir then bake uncovered for 35–40 minutes, turning the sausages and lentils over in the juices halfway through the cooking time.

pork and flageolet bean stew

Another winning dish that involves minimal preparation while giving the impression that it has taken ages! The frozen pork needs to be in individual pieces otherwise it won't cook evenly from frozen, so either buy the 'cook from frozen' bags or open freeze your pork chunks on a tray before bagging them up. If you prefer you can make this dish using fresh pork. Any leftovers can be frozen, defrosted and reheated at another time.

Serves 4

1 tablespoon vegetable oil

1 large onion, peeled and cut into
    wedges, or 3 good handfuls of frozen
    chopped onion

450g frozen cubes of pork leg, or fresh
    pork, cut into bite-sized pieces

4cm fresh ginger, peeled and chopped

1 large garlic clove, chopped

3 carrots, peeled and chopped

1 medium cooking apple, peeled,
    cored and sliced, or a handful frozen
    apple slices

100ml white wine

1 tablespoon Worcestershire sauce

3 tablespoons clear honey

1 tablespoon soy sauce

300ml vegetable stock

6 mushrooms, sliced, or 2 handfuls
    frozen mushroom slices

1 x 400g tin flageolet beans, drained
    and rinsed

1 large courgette, sliced

Preheat the oven to 150°C/140°C fan/gas mark 2. Heat the oil in a heavy-bottomed casserole and add the onion. Soften over a medium heat for 5 minutes. Increase the heat and add the pork. Stir-fry for 5 minutes, then add the ginger, garlic, carrot and apple and stir-fry for a further 5 minutes. Add the wine, Worcestershire sauce, honey, soy sauce and vegetable stock. Season, stir, bring to the boil, then cover and cook in the oven for an hour.

Remove the casserole from the oven and add the mushrooms, beans and courgette. Stir, cover the casserole and return to the oven for a further 30 minutes or until the pork is tender. Taste for seasoning and sweetness, then serve.

pork belly with crackling, fennel and shallots

1 piece boneless pork belly, weighing about 1.8–1.9kg once boned (about 2.3kg pre-boned weight), fat scored, frozen in a flat piece

3 rounded teaspoons sea salt flakes

1 teaspoon fennel seeds

zest of 1 lemon

350ml dry cider, plus a splash for the gravy

1 large fennel bulb, trimmed, cored and cut into wedges

5 medium-sized carrots, halved or quartered lengthways

12 shallots, peeled

3 garlic cloves, unpeeled but squashed with the back of a knife

200–400ml chicken stock

For the gravy

3 teaspoons runny honey

2 teaspoons soy sauce

To serve

steamed cabbage

mashed potatoes

Apple Sauce (see page 18)

Wonderful pork belly has got everything, as long as it's cooked slowly: tender meat with lots of flavour and crispy crackling. And cooking it from frozen is just brilliant! However, if cooking from fresh, just spread it with the lemony mixture before it goes in the oven, keep it skin side up from the start and miss out the initial cooking at the high temperature.

Serves 4–6

Preheat the oven to 230°C/220°C fan/gas mark 8.

Lay the pork belly skin side down on a rack inside a large roasting tin. Roast for 25 minutes on the top shelf of the oven. Meanwhile, using a pestle and mortar, pound half the salt with the fennel seeds, lemon zest and a good grinding of black pepper. Remove the pork from the oven, rub the lemony mixture all over the flesh, then carefully turn the meat over so that it is skin side up, and sprinkle over the rest of the salt, using the back of a spoon to rub it into the skin. Turn the oven down to 150°C/140°C fan/gas mark 2, pour the cider into the base of the roasting tin – not over the meat, or you won't get crackling – and return it to the oven, on the middle shelf, for 1 hour.

Then add the vegetables and garlic to the base of the tin, under the pork. Pour in 300ml chicken stock (avoiding the meat again) and cook for a further 1³/4 hours, or until the vegetables are just tender. Check occasionally to make sure there is sufficient liquid, adding more stock if necessary.

Remove the tin from the oven and increase the heat to 230°C/220°C fan/gas mark 7. Take the pork and rack out of the tin, sit it on another roasting tray and return to the oven for 20–30 minutes. (Then, if the crackling still hasn't developed, simply remove the fat and skin from the meat and carefully grill until bubbling and crisp). Meanwhile, using a slotted spoon, remove the vegetables to a warm dish, reserving the liquid. Cover and keep warm.

Remove the pork from the oven, transfer to a board, loosely cover with foil and rest. Put the vegetable roasting tin on the hob, pour in a splash of cider and stir over the heat. Add more chicken stock if you don't have enough liquid in your tin, along with the honey, soy sauce and a dollop of apple sauce, if using. Season and simmer for 10 minutes, then pour in any remaining pork juices and strain into a jug. Serve the pork with the roasted vegetables, cabbage, mashed potatoes, gravy, apple sauce and plenty of crackling!

prepare-ahead mains

beef wellington

splash of olive oil

900g piece of beef fillet, taken from the middle, with an even thickness of about 10cm

250g chestnut mushrooms, very finely chopped

1 large garlic clove, finely chopped

1 tablespoon Madeira

1 x 500g block all-butter puff pastry, defrosted

flour, for dusting

6 slices Parma ham

1/2 teaspoon English mustard powder

1 egg, beaten, for brushing

To serve

Madeira Sauce (see page 24)

buttered new potatoes

green beans or a green salad

The ideal main course for a special occasion – it looks as though you've been toiling all day when in fact you've been having your hair and nails done! Serve it with the Madeira Sauce on page 24.

Serves 4–6

Season the beef all over with black pepper. Add a splash of oil to a very hot heavy-based frying pan. When smoking, put the beef in and quickly brown it all over – about 5–10 seconds on each side, not forgetting the ends. Remove to a board to leave to cool completely.

Add the mushrooms to the pan and cook over a medium heat for about 5 minutes, letting them brown, but stirring occasionally. Add the garlic, stir for a minute, then add the Madeira and some salt and pepper and keep cooking until all the liquid has evaporated. Remove to a bowl and let cool.

Take the pastry from the fridge and roll out on a floured surface until 3–4mm thick. Cut to fit your piece of beef (I haven't given exact measurements as fillets can vary so enormously in size, but the pastry will need to be large enough to wrap up your beef, with a generous overlap). Lay 4 Parma ham slices side by side on the pastry so that they are touching, then spoon most of the mushroom mix over the ham and pat down. Sprinkle the beef with the mustard powder and rub all over, then place the fillet on top of the mushrooms in the centre of the pastry. Spoon over the remaining mushroom mix, pat down and lay the 2 final slices of Parma ham lengthways along the beef. Carefully and tightly bring the lower pieces of Parma ham up and over the beef to wrap it. Then trim the pastry, brush all the pastry edges with beaten egg and fold up to enclose the beef in the most dainty but efficient way you can. Place on a baking tray lined with greaseproof paper, with the pastry folds on the underside, and brush all over with beaten egg.

(F) Open freeze the beef on the lined baking tray. When frozen, carefully transfer into a bag and freeze until required.

(D) Leave for about 24 hours in the fridge before cooking.

(R) When ready to cook the beef, preheat the oven to 220°C/200°C fan/gas mark 7. Remove the beef from the fridge and place on a baking sheet. Leave for 20 minutes at room temperature, then bake in the oven for 30–35 minutes or until the pastry is golden brown. Rest for 5–10 minutes before slicing thickly and serving with Madeira Sauce (see page 24), buttered new potatoes and green beans or a green salad.

lamb and prune tagine

1 teaspoon coriander seeds
1 teaspoon cumin seeds
1/2 teaspoon paprika (hot)
1/2 teaspoon ground cinnamon
2 tablespoons olive oil
2 onions, cut into wedges
800g lamb neck fillet, cut into chunks
4 garlic cloves, crushed
300ml lamb stock
1 x 400g tin of tomatoes
300g sweet potatoes, peeled and cut
   into chunks
12 pitted ready-to-eat prunes
2 teaspoons runny honey
pinch of saffron threads, soaked in
   1 tablespoon water (optional)

To serve
herby couscous

I do like the combination of fruit, meat and spices with lots of lovely juice and buttery, herby couscous. This is a stew-like tagine using a cheap cut of meat. It's a favourite in our household – my baby has a mashed-up version!

Serves 4

Crush the coriander and cumin seeds using a pestle and mortar. Put into a bowl and stir in the paprika, cinnamon and half the oil. Add the lamb and stir so that it is thoroughly coated in the spice mix.

Heat the remaining 1 tablespoon oil in a flameproof casserole or heavy-based pan over a medium heat and fry the onions until just beginning to soften and brown. Add the lamb, turn up the heat and brown all over. Add the garlic and stir-fry for another 2 minutes, then pour in the stock and tomatoes. Season, cover and cook at a gentle simmer for an hour.

Add the potatoes, prunes, honey and saffron (if using) to the casserole and cook for a further 45 minutes, or until the lamb is tender.

(**F**) Pour into a container, cool, cover, label and freeze.

(**D**) Leave overnight in the fridge.

(**R**) Put the tagine into a pan, bring to the boil, then simmer gently for 15 minutes, or until piping hot. Serve with herby couscous.

fennel, leek and potato gratin

50g butter

2 fennel bulbs, trimmed and sliced

2 large leeks, sliced

1kg potatoes, peeled and cut into 3/4 cm slices

2 garlic cloves, crushed

300ml double cream

150ml milk

200g blue cheese (eg. Stilton), crumbled

Great for vegetarians, but also a cheery accompaniment to leftover cold roast meat. It's a real winner on Boxing Day!

Serves 6

In a large pan, melt the butter over a gentle heat, then add the fennel and leeks and stir-fry for 3–4 minutes. Add the potato and garlic and stir over the heat for a further 3 minutes, then pour in the cream and milk and season with pepper. Bring to a simmer then cook over a very gentle heat, stirring occasionally, for 20–25 minutes, or until the potatoes feel about half cooked. Stir in half the crumbled cheese, then transfer to a large ovenproof dish. Sprinkle over the remaining cheese.

(F) Cool, then cover with foil, label and freeze.

(R) Cook from frozen. Preheat the oven to 150°C/140°C fan/gas mark 2. Put the foil-covered baking dish in the oven and bake for 1–1 1/2 hours, or until soft when poked with a knife, and bubbling.

chicken with chorizo, peppers and olives

2 tablespoons olive oil

225g cooked chorizo sausage, casing removed, chopped

1kg skinless and boneless chicken thighs or breasts, cut into bite-sized pieces

1/2 teaspoon sweet paprika

splash of white wine

150g drained roasted red peppers, cut into strips

1/2 batch (700–800ml) All-purpose Tomato Sauce (see page 33)

2 rosemary sprigs

about 3 tablespoons pitted black olives

A quick-fix supper or one to freeze for when friends come over.

Serves 6–8

Heat the oil in a large deep frying pan and fry the chorizo until beginning to brown and release its oil. Remove to a plate. Add the chicken to the pan and brown over a high heat (you might need to do this in 2 batches). Return the chorizo to the pan with all the chicken and stir in the paprika. Add the wine and simmer for 2 minutes, then stir in the peppers, tomato sauce and rosemary and season to taste. Simmer for about 15 minutes, or until the chicken is just cooked through, then stir in the olives.

(F) Pour the chicken into containers, then cool, cover, label and freeze.

(D) Leave overnight in the fridge.

(R) Place in a saucepan over low heat, stirring occasionally, until piping hot.

chicken, taleggio and spinach pancakes

If you can't find Taleggio cheese, use Cheddar or Gruyère instead. You can also use fresh cooked and drained spinach if you prefer. Make a double batch of the Pancake mixture (see page 30) and freeze what you don't need – either the batter or the cooked pancakes – for later.

For the sauce
50g plain flour
50g butter
500ml milk
200g pack Taleggio cheese, chopped
    into 1–2cm pieces

For the filling
knob of butter
splash of oil
1 small onion, chopped
800g skinless and boneless chicken
    thighs, cut into small chunks
2 garlic cloves, crushed
350g mushrooms, cut into
    thickish slices
2 good pinches oregano
splash white wine
200g frozen whole leaf spinach cubes,
    cooked and drained
150ml chicken stock
8 cooked plain Pancakes (see page 30)

Makes 8 pancakes (serves 4)

To make the sauce, put the flour, butter and milk into a pan and whisk over a medium heat until thickened. Remove the pan from the heat and add half of the Taleggio and a grinding of black pepper. Stir with a wooden spoon until melted, then set aside.

To make the filling, heat the butter and oil in a pan and soften the onion gently for 5 minutes or so. Add the chicken and stir-fry with the onions until sealed. Add the garlic, mushrooms and oregano and cook for another 2 minutes, then pour in the wine. Bubble for a minute or so, then add about half of the cheese sauce, the spinach and the stock. Season and simmer for 2 minutes, then cool completely.

Divide the filling between the pancakes and roll up. Place the filled pancakes in a dish and top with the remaining cheese sauce, then scatter over the remaining Taleggio.

(**F**) Cover with cling film and foil, label and freeze.

(**D**) Leave overnight in the fridge.

(**R**) Preheat the oven to 180°C/160°C fan/gas mark 4. Cover the dish with foil and bake for 40–50 minutes or until piping hot, then brown under a hot grill.

chicken, ham and tarragon pie

1 x 500g block all-butter puff pastry,
  defrosted

flour, for dusting

2 thick slices of good-quality cooked
  ham, cut into strips

1 heaped tablespoon finely chopped
  fresh tarragon

1/2 quantity of Chicken with White
  Wine and Herbs (see page 35)

1 egg, beaten

The ultimate comforting supper, bursting with flavoursome vegetables and a rich herby gravy. You can either use some of the pre-frozen chicken filling (see page 35), in which case defrost it, then assemble the pie and eat straight away (not to be refrozen). Alternatively, you can make the filling, cool and assemble the pie, then freeze the whole thing uncooked, ready to defrost and cook at a later date.

Serves 4

Roll out the pastry on a floured surface and, using your pie dish as a template, cut out a piece to generously fit the top. From the trimmings, cut a 2cm wide strip (it can be in pieces) to fit around the rim of the dish. Dampen the edges and stick the strips in place around the rim.

Mix the ham and tarragon into the chicken filling then spoon this into the dish. Dampen the top of the pastry strip and place the pastry round on top. Trim the edges and press down gently. Decorate the top if you wish with pastry shapes made from the trimmings, then brush with the beaten egg and make a small slit in the top for a steam hole. Either freeze (if the filling hasn't already been frozen) or cook within 4 hours (keep the pie in the fridge).

(**F**) Cover the pie dish, label and freeze.

(**D**) Leave overnight in the fridge.

(**C**) Remove the pie from the fridge 20 minutes before cooking. Preheat the oven to 190°C/180°C fan/gas mark 5. Bake the pie for 30–35 minutes or until piping hot and deep golden.

crab cakes with citrus and avocado salad

450g potatoes, peeled and cut into
  large chunks
150g skinless cod or haddock fillet
150ml whole milk
25g butter
4 spring onions, trimmed and chopped
1 large clove garlic
1 heaped tablespoon plain flour
zest of 1 and juice 1/2 lime
2 pinches cayenne pepper
2 x 170g tin white crabmeat in
  brine, drained or 240g fresh white
  crabmeat (not previously frozen)
2 tablespoons fresh chopped coriander
5–6 tablespoons semolina
vegetables oil, for frying

For the citrus salad
1 avocado, peeled, destoned and sliced
1 orange, segmented
1 pink grapefruit, segmented
2–3 handfuls herb salad
1–2 tablespoons olive oil

I like the addition of a small amount of fish in these, purely because they add a little more texture and the poaching liquid gives the mixture a bit more depth of flavour. Use fresh crabmeat if you have it, just ensure it really is fresh meat, not some that has been frozen and defrosted.

Makes 12 small crab cakes (3 each or 2 for a starter)

Boil the potatoes in salted water until soft, then drain. Meanwhile bring the fish to a simmer in the milk, then simmer for a further 5 minutes, or until cooked through. Remove from the milk to a plate (reserving the milk in a jug). Melt the butter in a saucepan and fry the spring onions and garlic for 2 minutes. Stir in the flour, then gradually incorporate the poaching milk and bring up to the boil. Simmer for 2 minutes. Add the potato and using a potato masher, mash until smooth. Flake in the fish then stir in the lime zest and juice. Season with a sprinkle of salt, cayenne and ground black pepper and extra lime juice, to taste. When cool, stir in the crabmeat and coriander, then leave in the fridge for about an hour to cool completely. Sprinkle half the semolina onto a board. With wet hands, shape the cold fish mixture into 12 cakes and sit on the semolina. Sprinkle over the remaining semolina to coat and carefully transfer to a board or tray covered in greaseproof paper.

(**F**) Open freeze the cakes, then bag and label.

(**C**) Fry the cakes from frozen gently in the oil for 6-8 minutes each side until golden and piping hot. Mix the salad leaves with the avocado, orange, grapefruit, a drizzle of olive oil and some seasoning. Serve with the crab cakes.

aubergine and lentil moussaka

5 tablespoons olive oil

1 medium aubergine, cut into
   1cm slices

400g potatoes, peeled and cut into
   1cm slices

75g Cheddar, grated

For the vegetable and lentil sauce

1 medium onion, peeled and chopped

1 large courgette, chopped

1 red pepper, chopped

2 garlic cloves, crushed

1/2 teaspoon ground cinnamon

1 1/2 tablespoons tomato purée

splash of red wine (optional)

700ml jar passata with garlic
   and herbs

1 x 400g tin green lentils, rinsed
   and drained

1–2 pinches of caster sugar

For the ricotta sauce

300ml milk

50g butter

50g plain flour

good grating of nutmeg

250g pot of ricotta cheese

My stepmother, Wendy, is a fabulous cook, who has the knack of producing incredible food, from wherever, using whatever, in what seems like minutes! She made the tastiest moussaka for us on a wonderful holiday for my father's 60th birthday in Greece a few years ago. This is a veggie version!

Serves 4–6

Heat a tablespoon of oil in a frying pan and fry the aubergine slices in batches, on both sides, until browned and beginning to soften. Transfer to a plate lined with kitchen paper while you fry the rest. (Add a little more oil if necessary to prevent sticking, but wait until it is very hot before adding the aubergine slices or they will be soggy and oily.) Set to one side.

Meanwhile, make the vegetable and lentil sauce. In a clean pan, heat a tablespoon of oil and fry the onion for a couple of minutes. Add the chopped courgette and pepper and gently fry for about 5 minutes, then add the garlic and fry for a further 2 minutes, or until the vegetables begin to soften. Stir in the cinnamon and tomato purée and cook for a minute or so before adding the red wine, if using, and after a further minute or so, the passata. Simmer for 10 minutes, then stir in the lentils, sugar and seasoning.

Meanwhile parboil the potato slices in salted water for about 3 minutes or until half cooked. Drain and leave to cool slightly while you make the ricotta sauce. Put the flour, butter and milk into a pan and whisk over a medium heat. When thickened, season with salt, pepper and some grated nutmeg and leave to cool for 5 minutes, then whisk in the ricotta.

Pour half of the vegetable sauce into the base of a deep round casserole or dish with about a 3-litre capacity. Top with the potato slices in one layer, then spread over half of the ricotta sauce. Layer on half the aubergines, followed by the remaining vegetable sauce, the rest of the aubergine, and then the last of the ricotta sauce. Top with the grated cheese.

(F) Cool. Cover with foil or a lid, label and freeze.

(D) Leave for at least 24 hours in the fridge. Remove and thaw at room temperature if need be.

(C) Preheat the oven to 190°C/180°C fan/gas mark 5. Bake for 45–55 minutes or until piping hot and bubbling.

slow-roast shoulder of lamb

For the roast lamb

2 x 1.7kg frozen shoulders of lamb

3 tablespoons olive oil

6 large carrots, trimmed and cut into
5cm lengths

4 celery sticks, trimmed and cut into
5cm lengths

2 large onions, peeled and halved

2 garlic heads, halved widthways

2 anchovy fillets

3 rosemary sprigs

3 bay leaves

2 tablespoons tomato purée

800ml chicken stock

500ml white wine

For the gravy

1 heaped teaspoon redcurrant jelly

dash of soy sauce

To serve

roast potatoes or Fennel, Leek and
Potato Gratin (see page 84)

green vegetable of your choice

Yes, you really can cook a joint from frozen! However, if you are cooking a fresh joint, simply reduce the sizzling time at the higher temperature to 25 minutes at the beginning and slow roast for 3 hours rather than 5. I have suggested using two shoulders, to make life easier and save on energy: you can roast both, eat one straight away with a gratin, such as the one on page 84, and turn the second into the Smart Shepherd's Pie (see opposite) that you can store in the freezer for a later occasion – or even turn both into pies. Of course, if you prefer, you can just halve the recipe.

Serves 4–6

Take the shoulders from the freezer an hour before cooking and put into a large roasting tin. Preheat the oven to 220°C/210°C fan/gas mark 7.

Drizzle the lamb shoulders with the oil and season with salt and pepper. Roast for 35 minutes, then reduce the heat to 150°C/140°C fan/gas mark 2. Remove the lamb from the oven, lift the shoulders up and scatter the carrot, celery, onion, garlic, anchovies, rosemary and bay leaves underneath. Mix the tomato purée into the hot stock, then pour over the lamb along with the wine. Cover reasonably tightly with a layer of foil and bake for 5 hours.

Remove the lamb shoulders from the oven, and transfer one to a separate dish along with half the vegetables, garlic and juices. Leave to cool before chilling until completely cold.

For the roast, pour the remaining lamb juices into a small pan, carefully skimming off some of the fat from the top as you do so. Then squeeze out half a head of the garlic into the pan. Add the redcurrant jelly and soy sauce and simmer for a few minutes. Strain and serve with the carved lamb, the Fennel, Leek and Potato Gratin on page 84 or roast potatoes, the remaining carrots and onions from the roasting tin and a green vegetable.

smart shepherd's pie

1/2 quantity Slow-roast Shoulder
   of Lamb (see opposite), cooled
1kg potatoes, peeled
200ml milk
40g butter
good grating of nutmeg

Using the lamb shoulder (left) turns this recipe from everyday to special occasion. For even more variety try using a mix of potato and celeriac in the mash too. The Mince For All Occasions (page 34) is another filling you can use with this topping – just defrost and follow the same cooking instructions (make sure it's not refrozen though).

Serves 4–6

Remove as much of the surface fat as you can from the lamb shoulder, then transfer the lamb and vegetables to a dish and the juices to a jug.

Boil the potatoes until tender. Heat the milk and butter in a pan and add to the potatoes before mashing. Season with salt, pepper and nutmeg and cool completely.

Take all the meat off the bone and cut into bite-sized pieces, discarding any lumps of fat. Cut the vegetables into smaller chunks and squeeze out the garlic cloves into the juices. Top up the juices to 400ml with a little water or stock if necessary. Put the meat and vegetables into an ovenproof dish and pour over the gravy. Top with the mash.

(**F**) Cover the dish, label and freeze.

(**D**) Leave overnight in the fridge.

(**C**) Preheat the oven to 180°C/160°C fan/gas mark 4. Cook for 40–50 minutes, or until golden and bubbling.

smoked fish, crab and watercress tart

1/2 quantity Shortcrust Pastry
  (see page 28), or 375g pack ready-
  rolled shortcrust pastry sheet
225g fresh smoked cod or haddock
  fillet
400ml whole milk
2 eggs, beaten
knob of butter
1 medium leek, trimmed and chopped
2 tablespoons plain flour
1–2 pinches cayenne pepper
100g fresh white crabmeat
  (not previously frozen)
100g fresh brown crabmeat
  (not previously frozen)
50g trimmed watercress, chopped

I adore the combination of smoked fish and watercress, and the addition of some fresh crab makes this a perfect summer entertaining recipe. Do make sure to use fresh crabmeat that has not been previously frozen and defrosted.

Serves 6–8

You will need a round loose-bottomed tart case with a base measurement of 24cm and a depth of 2.5cm.

Preheat the oven to 190°C/180°C fan/gas mark 5. If using the block of pastry then roll the pastry out to a large circle on a floured surface. Line the tart case with the rolled out pastry or ready-rolled sheet and chill for 30 minutes. Scrunch up some greaseproof paper, put it into the tart case and fill with baking beans. Bake for 15 minutes.

Put the fish and milk into a dish, cover with foil and poach in the oven for 20 minutes. Remove the foil and transfer the fish onto a dish to cool, then flake. Reserve the poaching milk.

Remove the paper and beans from the tart and brush with a little of the beaten egg. Return the pastry case to the oven for a further 5 minutes.

Melt the butter in a pan and fry the leek gently until softened. Add the flour and stir. Gradually stir in the poaching milk and bring to the boil. Season with cayenne, salt and pepper. Simmer for 2–3 minutes, then put the pan into a sink a quarter full of cold water to help chill it down. When the sauce is completely cold, add the crab, flaked smoked cod, watercress and beaten eggs and stir carefully before pouring it into the tart case.

(F) Cover the uncooked tart, still in its tin, with cling film, then freeze. When frozen, carefully remove from the tin and transfer to a bag.

(D) When ready to cook, place the tart back in the tin and defrost overnight in the fridge.

(C) Preheat the oven to 180°C/160°C fan/gas mark 4. Put a baking sheet in the oven to heat (heating the tray will ensure the pastry isn't soggy). Put the tart on the hot baking sheet and cook for 30–40 minutes until just set and golden. Leave to rest for a few minutes before serving.

aromatic lamb curry

2 good splashes vegetable oil
5cm cinnamon stick
12 cloves
12 cardamon pods
3 teaspoons cumin seeds
3 onions, finely diced
12 garlic cloves, crushed
7cm piece of fresh ginger, peeled and
   finely grated
2 x 400g tins chopped tomatoes
3 green chillies, slit (seeds removed
   if you prefer a less fiery curry)
3/4 teaspoon hot chilli powder
1 heaped teaspoon flaked sea salt
1.5kg lamb, cut into chunks

To serve
large handful of chopped coriander
dhal or rice
naan breads
steamed green beans tossed with
   butter and black onion seeds

Curry Queen Sheila Damodaran gave me her recipe for a quick-to-prepare lamb curry to include in this book, as she is passionate about cooking healthy Indian food for families. This works best with diced lamb shoulder but would be fine with diced leg too. As it is a reasonably dry curry, serve it with dhal and naan breads.

Serves 4

Heat the oil in a heavy saucepan and add the whole spices. When they begin to sizzle, add the onions and fry until golden brown in colour – around 8 minutes. Add the garlic and ginger and cook for another minute or so.

Add the tomatoes, whole chillies, chilli powder and salt and cook for about 10–12 minutes until the sauce is thick.

Add the meat and bring to the boil, then pour in 200ml of boiling water and reduce the heat until barely simmering. (The secret of a very tender meat curry is never to let it boil vigorously.) Cook for 1 1/2–2 hours, or until very tender, with the lid resting on the top. Check occasionally that the curry is not becoming too dry and add a little extra water if necessary.

(F) Cool, then pour into freezer containers, label and freeze.

(D) Leave overnight in the fridge.

(R) Put the curry into a pan, bring to the boil, then simmer gently for 15 minutes or until piping hot. Add the coriander and serve with some dhal or rice, naan breads and some steamed green beans tossed with butter and black onion seeds.

beef and spinach lasagne

50g butter
50g plain flour
450ml milk
300g frozen leaf spinach cubes
75g mature Cheddar, grated
50g Parmesan, grated
grated nutmeg
1/4 batch Mince For All Occasions
   (see page 34)
6–8 lasagne sheets

Lasagne is a favourite with most families and this version uses the Mince For All Occasions on page 34. Either make the lasagne using freshly made and cooled mince (before it has been frozen) and freeze the prepared dish uncooked, or defrost a container of the Mince For All Occasions, prepare the lasagne and cook it straight away. But don't defrost the mince sauce, assemble the lasagne and then refreeze. If you are cooking for larger numbers, just double the quantities and prepare in a larger dish. It might need an extra 10 minutes in the oven just to ensure the middle gets piping hot. You can use fresh spinach if you prefer, just stir the cooked and drained spinach into the hot white sauce.

Serves 4

First make the sauce. Melt the butter in a pan over a gentle heat, stir in the flour and cook for 2 minutes. Gradually incorporate the milk and bring to the boil. Then stir in the frozen spinach cubes and simmer until defrosted. Remove the pan from the heat, mix the cheeses together and add half to the sauce. Stir until the cheese has melted and season with grated nutmeg and salt and pepper. Leave to cool.

When the sauce is cool, assemble the lasagne. Put half the mince in the base of a 2-litre lasagne dish, top with about 3 sheets of lasagne, then spread over just under half of the spinach sauce. Lay another 3 sheets of lasagne over the top, then spoon over the remainder of the meat sauce and finish with the remainder of the spinach sauce. Scatter over the remaining cheese. Either cook (if using defrosted mince) or freeze (if using freshly-made mince) at this point.

(D) Leave overnight in the fridge.

(C) Preheat the oven to 180°C/160°C fan/gas mark 4. Cook the lasagne for 35–45 minutes, or until golden, bubbling and piping hot.

ox cheeks with red wine and mushrooms

25g pack mixed dried mushrooms
  (I used porcini, oyster and shiitake)

3 heaped tablespoons plain flour

1.7kg ox cheeks, cut in half

2–3 tablespoons vegetable oil or a knob
  of beef dripping

4 thick slices of smoked streaky bacon,
  chopped

2 red onions, peeled and cut into
  wedges

2 celery sticks, trimmed and sliced

2 garlic cloves, crushed

1^1/$_2$ tablespoons tomato purée

2 tablespoons redcurrant jelly

400ml full-bodied red wine

2 bay leaves

1 rosemary sprig

415g tin beef consommé, or 400ml
  beef stock if you have it

To serve

knob of butter

6 large Portobello mushrooms, sliced

2 tablespoons fresh parsley, chopped

creamy celeriac and potato mash or
  dauphinoise potatoes

green leafy vegetable

Don't let the cut of meat put you off – once you have tried these, I'm sure you will love them. However it is also delicious made with stewing steak.

Serves 6–8

Soak the dried mushrooms in a jug with 200ml hot water for 30 minutes. Preheat the oven to 150°C/140°C fan/gas mark 2. Season the flour with plenty of salt and pepper, then toss the ox cheeks in the flour until coated.

Heat 1 tablespoon of oil (or beef dripping) in a large heavy-based frying pan. Add the bacon and cook until just crisp. Transfer to a plate and set aside.

Add a little more oil or dripping to the pan and heat until smoking. Add about half the floured ox cheeks (you don't want the pan to be crowded) and cook for about 3 minutes until they are really brown, pushing down on them using a fish slice to help them brown faster. Turn them over and brown the other sides and edges. Transfer to a casserole then cook the remaining cheeks in the same way, adding a little extra oil if needed.

Once you have added the last of the cheeks to the casserole, turn the heat down under the frying pan, add the onions and celery and soften gently for about 10 minutes. Squeeze the liquid from the soaked dried mushrooms into a bowl and reserve, then add the mushrooms and garlic to the onions and celery. Cook for a further 2 minutes, then raise the heat, stir in the tomato purée, redcurrant jelly and red wine and bubble for 3 minutes before adding to the casserole, along with the bacon, herbs and consommé or beef stock and mushroom soaking liquid. Cover and cook in the oven for 3 hours.

(**F**) Using a slotted spoon, remove the meat and vegetables to a container. Taste and season the sauce, adding salt, pepper or redcurrant jelly if needed, then pour over the meat. Cool, cover with a lid, label and freeze.

(**D**) Leave for at least 24 hours in the fridge.

(**R**) Preheat the oven to 180°C/160°C fan/gas mark 4. Melt the butter in a frying pan and fry the mushrooms for 3–4 minutes. Return the meat, vegetables and sauce to a flameproof casserole. Add the mushrooms, bring to a simmer, cover and put in the oven for 25 minutes. Reduce the heat to 150°C/140°C fan/gas mark 2 and cook for 45 minutes. Sprinkle with parsley and serve with mash or dauphinoise potatoes and greens.

teatime treats

quick double-chocolate tray bake

200g butter, softened
200g caster sugar
4 large eggs
25g cocoa, dissolved in
    3–4 tablespoons boiling water
    to make a smooth paste
200g self-raising flour
1/2 teaspoon baking powder
100g dark chocolate chips
smarties, chocolate buttons or fresh
    raspberries, to decorate

For the icing
1 tablespoon cocoa, dissolved in
    2 tablespoons boiling water to
    make a smooth paste
75g butter, softened
200g icing sugar

Pooh, my mother-in-law, makes the best easy family-style chocolate cake, which we persuade her to make whenever there's a birthday! Her secret is dissolving the cocoa in boiling water before adding it. If you prefer a more traditional cake, you can divide this between two round tins and fill.

Makes 12–14 pieces

Preheat the oven to 180°C/160°C fan/gas mark 4. Grease and line a 28 x 18 x 5cm tray bake tin.

Put the softened butter, sugar, eggs and dissolved cocoa into a large bowl. Sieve over the flour and baking powder. Using a hand-held electric whisk, beat the mixture until it is pale and creamy – about 2 minutes. Using a metal spoon, fold in the chocolate chips.

Turn the mixture into the greased tin and spread it out evenly. Bake for 30–35 minutes, or until risen and springy to the touch. Cool slightly before turning onto a wire rack.

Once the cake is cool, whisk the icing ingredients together in a bowl and spread over the cake. Run a fork across the surface of the icing to create a wavy pattern of lines.

(F) Place the iced cake on a tray or plate and open freeze. Once frozen, place into a box or freezer bag and return to the freezer.

(D) Leave overnight on a cooling rack, then sprinkle with topping of choice.

freezer biscuits

375g plain flour
1 rounded teaspoon baking powder
150g caster sugar
250g butter, softened
1 large egg, beaten
1 teaspoon vanilla extract

For the decoration (optional)
icing sugar
lemon juice (or water)
food colouring and/or edible
   decorations

These are just what freezer biscuits should be: versatile, melt in the mouth and child-proof – they can roll out the dough countless times and it will still taste good! I've given some flavour variations but you can devise others – the possibilities are endless! I tend to use some of the mixture straight away, then freeze the rest for later. My friend Anna inspired me to include these as she has a great Scandinavian recipe for lemon biscuits, which she often makes with her son Sasha – a great activity for a rainy day!

Makes about 40 biscuits

Sift the flour, baking powder and a pinch of salt together in a bowl. Put the butter and sugar into another bowl and beat using a hand-held electric whisk until combined. Add the dry ingredients, egg and vanilla extract and beat again. Using floured hands, form the mixture into a ball. If cooking and eating straight away, follow the instructions below to roll the mixture into 2 sausage shapes and slice into 1cm thick slices. Cook as per below. Alternatively choose one of the following three options:

Freeze, slice and bake

Divide the mixture into 2 equal portions and, using your hands, roll each out on a floured surface to form a sausage shape measuring about 4–5cm in diameter. Wrap each sausage in cling film and freeze. When you are ready to bake the biscuits, remove from the freezer about 15 minutes before, then slice into 1cm thick slices and cook as per below.

Cut into shapes, freeze then bake

Form the mixture into a ball, wrap in cling film and chill for 20 minutes. Roll out on a floured surface to about 1cm thickness, use cookie cutters to cut into shapes and freeze the uncooked biscuits between sheets of greaseproof paper. Bake from frozen as needed.

Cut into shapes, bake then freeze

Cut out shapes as above, bake, then freeze the cooked biscuits and defrost on a wire rack as needed.

(C) Preheat the oven to 180°C/160°C fan/gas mark 4. Place a sheet of baking paper on a baking tray then space the biscuits 1–2cm apart on the paper. Bake for 12–18 minutes, depending on whether or not you are cooking them from frozen (they should be just starting to take on colour around the edges when ready). Transfer to a cooling rack to cool completely.

To ice: If you like you can ice the biscuits. Just mix some icing sugar with a few drops of water or lemon juice and blend until smooth and just pourable (mix in a little food colouring at this point if you like). Drizzle or spread the icing over the biscuits, once cooled, and top with sprinkles or other edible decorations as you wish.

Variations:

Each of the following variations uses a half quantity of freezer biscuit mixture. You can split the dough into 2 equal portions in 2 separate bowls and use a wooden spoon to mix in the additional ingredients.

Pistachio – Mix in 2 tablespoons of shelled, chopped pistachio nuts. Form into a sausage or roll out as per recipe opposite. Alternatively, simply press the chopped nuts into the side of plain biscuits before baking.

Chocolate orange – Mix in 1 tablespoon of sifted cocoa powder and the zest of 1 large orange. (This gives a subtle orange flavour – add more zest for a stronger orange taste.) Form into a sausage or roll out as per recipe opposite.

Oat and sultana – Mix in 50g porridge oats and 2 heaped tablespoons of sultanas. Form into a sausage or roll out as per recipe opposite.

Honey and almond – Replace 25g of the sugar with 2 teaspoons of well-flavoured honey and add 2 tablespoons of toasted flaked almonds. Form into a sausage or roll out as per recipe opposite.

healthier flapjacks

150g butter
100g Demerara sugar
100g golden syrup
250g porridge oats
100g bag dried mixed berries
1 eating apple, peeled, cored and grated
1¹/₂ tablespoons sesame seeds

I often put a frozen bar in my son William's lunchbox and it is always defrosted in time for his lunch. These are a healthier alternative to normal flapjacks, but without the taste and texture of cardboard! Personally, I don't really see the point in making occasional treats if they are so packed with 'healthy' things that they no longer taste nice!

Makes 15 bars

Preheat the oven to 180°C/160°C fan/gas mark 4. Grease a 22 x 18cm baking tray and line it with greaseproof paper. (I always leave some paper hanging over the edges of the tin, as it acts as a good handle when lifting out the cooled slab.)

Heat the butter, sugar and golden syrup gently in a pan until the butter has melted and the sugar is beginning to dissolve.

Put the porridge oats, dried mixed berries, grated apple and sesame seeds into a bowl and stir together, then pour over the hot butter, sugar and syrup mixture and mix thoroughly. Turn the mixture into the greased and lined tin and bake for 20–25 minutes.

Leave to cool for 10 minutes, before cutting into 15 bars in the tin. When cold, remove the slab from the tin and layer the bars between sheets of greaseproof paper in a plastic container.

(**F**) Cover the container, then label and freeze.

(**D**) Leave at room temperature for 2–3 hours.

buttercream sponge

225g very soft butter
225g golden caster sugar
4 large eggs, beaten
2 level teaspoons baking powder
4 tablespoons orange juice or milk
225g self-raising flour

For the filling
100g soft butter
75g cream cheese
175g icing sugar, plus a little for
    dusting
1 teaspoon vanilla extract with seeds
4–5 tablespoons soft set raspberry
    or strawberry jam

I was taught cookery at school by Mrs Wilkinson and Mrs Jackson. I can still hear the latter shouting out in her Yorkshire accent 'don't forget to greeeeze your baking trays'. They taught me that the simplest way to make a sponge is by using the imperial measurements, as it is then the same number in ounces (in this case 8oz) of soft butter, sugar and flour with half the quantity of eggs (ie. 4 eggs) – an easy rule for children to remember too. I've added cream cheese to the filling to make it a little less sickly, but you can make a normal butter cream or use thick cream if you prefer.

Serves 8–10

Preheat the oven to 190°C/170°C fan/gas mark 5. Grease one loose-bottomed tin measuring 20cm across and 9cm deep.

If you want to save time, you can put all the sponge ingredients into an electric mixer, sieving over the flour and baking powder last. Then whizz for about 2 minutes until it's well combined, turn it into the tin and bake.

Alternatively (which I think gives the better result), put the soft butter and sugar into a large bowl. Using an electric hand whisk, or wooden spoon if you have good arm muscles, beat until it is light and pale and creamy – about 2 minutes. Add the egg, bit by bit, beating well, as well as a tablespoon of the flour towards the end to stop it curdling.

Then remove the whisk and sieve over the flour and baking powder. Using a large metal spoon fold lightly until combined, adding the orange juice or milk towards the end. Pour into the cake tin and lightly spread out. Put into the centre of the oven and bake for 40–45 minutes or until springy to the touch and a skewer comes out clean when inserted. Let it cool slightly then remove to a cooling rack to cool completely.

Meanwhile beat the butter, cream cheese, sugar and extract until combined. Halve the cake horizontally across the middle and spread the base with the butter cream. Lightly spread over the jam and top with the second cake.

(**F**) Open freeze, then carefully put into a bag, label and freeze.

(**D**) Leave on a cooling rack for 5–6 hours. Dust with icing sugar before serving.

st clement's drizzle cake

175g soft butter
200g caster sugar
zest of 1 orange
zest of 1 lemon
3 large eggs
200g self-raising flour, sifted
100ml whole milk
1 teaspoon baking powder, sifted

For the syrup
100g caster sugar
juice of 1 lemon
juice of 1/2 orange

I always think of summer when I think of St Clement's: the bright colours of orange and yellow evoke a feeling of warm sunny days. This cake is zingy and fresh tasting – and an easy one to throw together.

Makes 12 squares

Preheat the oven to 180°C/160°C fan/gas mark 4. Grease and line a 24 x 20 x 5cm tray bake tin.

Put the butter, the 200g of caster sugar and the orange and lemon zest into a bowl and beat using a hand-held electric whisk until pale and fluffy. Beat in the eggs, one at a time, then add about half the flour and half the milk. Whisk until incorporated, then add the remaining flour and milk and the baking powder and whisk again.

Pour the mixture into the greased and lined tray bake tin and spread out. Bake for 30–35 minutes, or until golden and springy to the touch. Remove from the oven and leave to cool for 5 minutes while you prepare the syrup.

Mix together the 100g of sugar with the lemon and orange juice. Carefully remove the cake from the tin, transferring it to a sheet of foil on a board. Pierce the top of the cake all over with a skewer, then lift up the edges of the foil to ensure no syrup escapes while you drizzle it all over. Leave to cool completely.

(**F**) Transfer the cake on the board to the freezer. Open freeze then remove the board and wrap in foil.

(**D**) Leave at room temperature for 4 hours.

blueberry, almond and orange cupcakes

110g butter, softened
110g caster sugar
2 eggs
50g ground almonds
zest of 1/2 small orange plus
  2 tablespoons juice
110g self-raising flour
1 teaspoon baking powder
100g blueberries

To serve
icing sugar, for dusting

I love baking with my three-year-old, William, though it tends to end up with me desperately trying to get the mixture in the tins before it's eaten! Blueberries are a favourite of his: indeed, as I write this, there's a little purple mouth smiling up at me – he has just gobbled the remaining blueberries in the packet! Blueberries also freeze beautifully: if you get the urge to bake, you can simply take them from the freezer and thaw them for about 30 minutes while you prepare the mixture.

Makes 15

You will need 2 cupcake trays and at least 15 paper cupcake cases

Preheat the oven to 190°C/180°C fan/gas mark 5. Put the butter, sugar, eggs, almonds and orange zest and juice into a bowl. Sieve over the flour and baking powder. Using a hand-held electric whisk, beat until smooth and fluffy – about 2 minutes. Fold in the blueberries and spoon into 2 cupcake trays filled with cases. Bake for 15–20 minutes.

(F) Cool on a wire rack then open freeze before packing into bags and labelling.

(D) Thaw them on a wire rack to prevent them going soggy. Dust with icing sugar before serving.

sultana scones

225g self-raising flour
1 1/2 rounded teaspoons baking powder
50g butter, chilled, diced
2 tablespoons caster sugar
3 tablespoons sultanas
7–8 tablespoons whole milk
2 teaspoons lemon juice
1 large egg, beaten

Scones freeze very well and are a lovely occasional treat to have to hand. I love sultana scones warmed through and buttered, but you can go all out and serve them with clotted cream and jam if you feel like a real feast! If you don't have a pastry cutter you can cut them into squares using a knife.

Makes 6–8

You will need a 6cm fluted pastry cutter.

Preheat the oven to 220°C/200°C fan/gas mark 7. Sift the flour and baking powder into a bowl and stir in a pinch of salt. Using the tips of your fingers, rub in the butter, lifting the flour to aerate it as you do so. Stir in the sugar and sultanas.

Mix 7 tablespoons of milk with the lemon and egg and stir nearly all of it into the flour mixture using a table knife (you need a little drop for brushing the tops). Add a little extra milk if needed to form a stiff dough.

Turn the dough onto a lightly floured surface and pat out gently to a square about 3cm tall. Use a 6cm fluted cutter to stamp out the scones (if you dip the cutter into a little flour first it will cut through the dough more easily). Alternatively cut into squares using a knife. Brush the tops of the scones with the remaining egg mixture. Use a palette knife to transfer the scones to a baking tray lined with greaseproof paper. Bake for 10–12 minutes or until risen and golden brown. Cool on a wire rack.

(**F**) Place in a freezer bag, label and freeze.

(**D**) Leave at room temperature for 1–2 hours on a wire rack.

(**R**) Preheat the oven to 180°C/160°C fan/gas mark 4 and bake for 5–8 minutes.

Variation:

Blueberry scones – Replace the sultanas with 3 tablespoons of dried blueberries.

bacon, cheddar and sunflower squares

4 slices smoked streaky bacon,
  finely chopped
250g self-raising wholemeal or light
  brown flour, sifted
1/2 teaspoon salt
1/2 teaspoon English mustard powder
1 teaspoon baking powder
25g butter, chilled, diced
100g Cheddar, grated
7–8 tablespoons whole milk
1 large egg, beaten
approx 2 teaspoons sunflower seeds

These are a cross between a scone and soda bread in taste and are lovely served up next to a bowl of soup or popped into the oven for a quick snack.

Makes 9

Preheat the oven to 220°C/200°C fan/gas mark 7. Dry fry the bacon in a small frying pan until crisp, then remove to a plate lined with kitchen paper.

In a large bowl, stir together the flour, salt, mustard powder and baking powder, then add the butter. Using the tips of your fingers, rub in the butter, lifting the flour to aerate it as you do so. Stir in the Cheddar and the bacon.

Mix 7 tablespoons of milk and the beaten egg together and pour nearly all of it into the mixture. Using a table knife, mix until combined. Add extra milk if needed to form a stiff dough.

Turn out onto a floured surface and form into a square shape about 3cm tall. Cut into 9 squares. Brush the tops of the squares with the remaining egg mixture, scatter with the sunflower seeds and place on a baking tray lined with greaseproof paper. Bake for about 15–18 minutes, or until risen and golden.

(F) Cool on a wire rack then place into a freezer bag, label and freeze.

(D) Leave for 1–2 hours at room temperature on a wire rack.

(R) Place in an oven preheated to 180°C/160°C fan/gas mark 4 for 5–10 minutes, or until warm.

choca-mocha loaf with mascarpone icing

200g butter, softened

200g golden caster sugar

4 eggs

2 teaspoons espresso coffee powder
dissolved in 1 tablespoon hot water

225g self-raising flour

1 teaspoon baking powder

1 tablespoon cocoa mixed with
2 tablespoons hot water

For the icing

75g mascarpone

50g butter

1 teaspoon espresso powder mixed
with 2 teaspoons hot water

250g icing sugar, sieved

To serve

cocoa, for dusting

toasted walnut pieces

**For those who find chocolate cake a bit too sickly and coffee cake not
sickly enough, this choca-mocha loaf is perfect!**

Serves 8

Preheat the oven to 180°C/160°C fan/gas mark 4. Grease and line a
900g loaf tin.

Put the butter, sugar, eggs, coffee mixture, flour and baking powder into a
bowl and, using a hand-held electric whisk, beat for about 2 minutes until
pale and creamy. Transfer half of the mixture into a second bowl and mix
in the cocoa mixture. Spoon dollops of the two mixtures randomly into the
prepared loaf tin, then level the top. Bake for 45–55 minutes until risen and
a skewer inserted into the cake comes out clean. Leave to cool for about 5
minutes in the tin then turn out onto a wire rack to cool completely.

Beat together the icing ingredients then spread over the top of the cooled
cake. (If the mixture is a little too runny, just put into the fridge to stiffen up
for 10 minutes or so.)

(F) Open freeze, then carefully put into a freezer bag.

(D) Leave overnight, then dust with cocoa and scatter with toasted walnuts
to serve.

easy mince pies

I have to admit, my family wouldn't care if I never made another mince pie again. However, I'm a traditionalist and feel drawn to making them at Christmas time, even though I'll probably be the only one eating them and will end up feeling like Father Christmas at the end of his rounds!

Makes 16

500g (1/2 quantity) homemade Sweet
   Pastry (see page 28) or 500g block
   all-butter shortcrust pastry
400g jar of good-quality mincemeat
a little milk
1 egg, beaten
caster sugar, for sprinkling

You will need 2 x 12 hole cupcake trays and 6cm and 7.5cm fluted pastry cutters.

Preheat the oven to 190°C/180°C fan/gas mark 5. Roll out the pastry on a floured surface until it is really thin (or you will end up with just pastry and no filling). Using the 7.5cm fluted pastry cutter, cut 16 rounds (you might get a couple more, depending on how efficient you've been with your rolling), then the same again using the slightly smaller cutter.

Line the cupcake holes with the larger pastry circles. Spoon a heaped teaspoon of mincemeat into each pastry case and brush the pastry edges with milk. Top with the smaller pastry rounds and press down around the edges to seal. Using the point of a knife or scissors, make two little slits in the top of each. Bake for 25–30 minutes or until golden.

(F) Cool the mince pies in the tin, then transfer them to a container between layers of greaseproof paper.

(R) Preheat the oven to 190°C/180°C fan/gas mark 5. Place the frozen pies on a baking tray and reheat for 8–10 minutes.

raspberry and white chocolate muffins

180ml whole milk
1 large egg
2 tablespoons vegetable oil
1/2 teaspoon vanilla extract with seeds
250g self-raising flour
150g golden caster sugar
100g white chocolate chunks
100g raspberries

To serve
icing sugar, for dusting

Great to make with little ones, these muffins couldn't be simpler and are delicious eaten warm or at room temperature. Sultanas, blueberries, dark chocolate and pecans are some of the other ingredients you could add to the basic mixture – just experiment with what you fancy!

Makes 12

You will need a 12-hole muffin tin and paper muffin cases (or a silicone muffin tray).

Preheat the oven to 190°C/180°C fan/gas mark 5. Combine the milk, egg, oil and vanilla in a jug and beat. Sift the flour into a bowl and stir in the sugar, a pinch of salt, the chocolate chunks and raspberries. Make a well in the centre and pour in the liquids. Using a fork, stir gently to combine (don't over stir or the muffins won't rise).

Place the muffin cases into the muffin tin and spoon the mixture into the cases. Bake for 20–25 minutes or until golden and risen. Leave to cool in the tin for 5 minutes, then remove to a wire rack to cool completely.

(**F**) Open freeze on a tray, then place into a plastic bag, label and return to the freezer.

(**D**) Place on a cooling rack for 4–5 hours, then eat as they are or warm in a low oven. Dust with icing sugar to serve.

puddings

nutty honeycomb ice cream

75g pecan nuts

vegetable oil, for greasing

110g golden caster sugar

3 tablespoons golden syrup

1 teaspoon bicarbonate of soda

2 teaspoons vanilla extract with seeds

1 litre double cream

1 x 405g can light or normal condensed milk

This recipe is an adaptation of a family favourite recipe for honeycomb ice cream, handed down to my sister-in-law Katie from her mum. The addition of nuts makes this my favourite type of ice cream! Eat it within a couple of weeks as it tends to lose its texture if you leave it for too long.

Makes 2.5 litres

Preheat the oven to 190°C/180°C fan/gas mark 5. Roughly break the pecan nuts in your hands, spread them out on a baking tray and place in the oven for 5 minutes, or until toasted. Remove from the oven and leave to cool.

Oil a sheet of greaseproof paper and place on a baking tray. Put the sugar and golden syrup in a saucepan and heat gently, swirling the pan until the sugar melts. Turn up the heat and boil for a few minutes until it turns a rich caramel colour, watching the mixture all the time to avoid it burning (it will take approximately 4 minutes). Remove the pan from the heat, then add the nuts and very carefully sprinkle in the bicarbonate of soda. It will suddenly look frothy and increase in volume. Stir, then pour quickly (before it sets) onto the oiled greaseproof paper. Allow to cool and set. Transfer to a plastic bag and bash with a rolling pin to break it into smallish chunks.

Using an electric whisk, whip the cream and vanilla extract in a large bowl until thickened slightly – it should be floppy, but should not have reached peaks stage. Then, with the whisk still running, pour in the condensed milk. Continue whisking until just stiff. Fold in the pieces of nutty honeycomb plus any crumbs.

(**F**) Turn into a 3-litre container and freeze for 6–8 hours.

(**S**) Remove from the freezer 20 minutes before you want to eat it and let it start to thaw in a cool place.

Tip: You might need to fill your saucepan with water once you have poured out the honeycomb mixture and bring it to the boil to remove the caramel.

no-churn vanilla ice cream

600ml double cream
405g can light or normal condensed
  milk
400ml freshly-made Custard (see page
  30), cooled, or 500g pot shop-bought
  fresh custard with vanilla seeds
1^1/$_2$ teaspoons vanilla extract
  with seeds

**If you are ice-cream lovers like my family and me, then you'll appreciate
the simplicity of this recipe – especially the fact you don't have to churn it!
Eat it within a couple of weeks as it tends to lose its texture if you leave it
for too long.**

Makes 1.5 litres

Using an electric whisk, whip the cream in a large bowl until floppy. With
the whisk still running, beat in the condensed milk, custard and vanilla
extract. Continue beating for about a minute.

(F) Pour into a 2-litre freezer container and seal with a lid.

(S) Remove from the freezer 20 minutes before you want to eat it and let it
start to thaw in a cool place.

eton mess ice cream

400g ripe strawberries

3 tablespoons good quality
strawberry jam

400ml double cream

1/2 x 405g can light or normal
condensed milk

4 meringues or meringue nests,
crushed in your hands

The addition of the jam seems odd, but it really intensifies the strawberry flavour. Eat this within a couple of weeks as it tends to lose its texture if you leave it for too long.

Makes 1.75 litres

Put the strawberries and jam into a blender and whizz until puréed. Using an electric whisk, whip the cream in a large bowl until floppy. With the beaters still going, beat in the condensed milk and then the strawberry purée. Continue beating until just stiff but still pourable, then fold in the crushed meringues.

(**F**) Pour into a 2-litre freezer container and seal with a lid.

(**S**) Remove from the freezer 20 minutes before you want to eat it and let it start to thaw in a cool place.

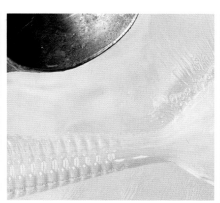

rhubarb crunch ice cream

500g rhubarb, fresh or frozen, cut into chunks (no need to defrost)
4 tablespoons caster sugar
2 tablespoons fresh orange juice

For the crunch
75g plain flour
50g butter, chilled, diced
3 tablespoons light muscovado sugar

For the ice cream base
600ml whipping cream
1 x 405g can light or normal condensed milk

I couldn't decide whether this was a cheesecake or a crumble, so decided it would be a crunch! Avoid tough, very green rhubarb as it just doesn't have the same flavour. Eat it within a couple of weeks as it tends to lose its texture if you leave it for too long.

Makes 1.8 litres

Preheat the oven to 180°C/160°C fan/gas mark 4. Put the rhubarb in a baking tin and sprinkle over the sugar and orange juice. Cover with foil and bake for 25 minutes or until softened.

Meanwhile, make the crunch. In a bowl, rub the flour and butter together, then stir in the sugar. Spread out onto a 24 x 20cm tin, so that it is about 1cm thick, and press down. Bake for about 20 minutes. Remove both fruit and crunch from the oven when cooked and leave to cool in their tins.

Using an electric whisk, beat the cream in a large bowl until floppy. With the whisk still running, add the condensed milk and any rhubarb cooking juice. Fold in the cooled rhubarb and beat again until thickened but still pourable. Roughly break up the crumble base and fold in, leaving some nice chunky bits.

(**F**) Turn into a 2-litre freezer container and freeze.

(**S**) Remove from the freezer 20 minutes before serving.

black and red ice cream

275g blackcurrants
175g redcurrants
4 tablespoons sloe gin or apple juice
1 1/2 x 405g cans light or normal
    condensed milk
750ml double cream
4 meringues, lightly crushed (optional)

I thought it would be nice to make an ice cream with redcurrants as they seem to be overlooked for desserts. You could make this with just blackcurrants if you like, but a mixture works better than redcurrants on their own. The fruits can be cooked from frozen if you have not bought them fresh. Eat it within a couple of weeks as it tends to lose its texture if you leave it for too long.

Makes 2 litres

Put the blackcurrants, redcurrants, gin or juice into a pan and simmer for 5–10 minutes, stirring every so often. Then, when they look like they have more or less burst, strain the berries through a sieve over a bowl and, using a spatula, squish all the purée through. Let the purée cool.

Using an electric whisk, beat the cream until floppy, then whisk in the condensed milk and berry purée. Using a spoon, fold in the meringue (if using) and turn into a 2-litre container.

(F) Place in the freezer for at least 4–5 hours, or until frozen.

(S) Remove from the freezer 20 minutes before serving.

black and red terrine

275g blackcurrants
175g redcurrants
4 tablespoons sloe gin or crème de cassis
1¹/₂ x 405g tins light or normal condensed milk
750ml double cream
4 meringues, lightly crushed

This is a more glamorous twist on the previous ice cream, and the great news is it doesn't need churning, so you can whip it up in the morning and forget about it until you are ready to serve it. The addition of a slug of booze adds an extra dimension, but you can use just water or apple juice if you prefer. Eat it within a couple of weeks as it tends to lose its texture if you leave it for too long.

Makes 2 x 900g terrines

You will need two 900g loaf tins.

Put the blackcurrants, redcurrants and sloe gin or crème de cassis into a pan with 2 tablespoons of water and simmer for 5–10 minutes, stirring every so often. When the currants have all more or less burst, strain them through a sieve over a bowl, using a spatula to push all the purée through.

Using an electric whisk, beat the cream until floppy, then whisk in the condensed milk and fruit purée. Using a spoon, fold in the meringue and turn the mixture into 2 non-stick (or cling film-lined) 900g loaf tins.

(**F**) Place in the freezer for at least 4–5 hours, or until frozen.

(**S**) Remove 20 minutes or so before eating and leave in a cool place. Turn out onto a plate, dipping the tins into warm water if sticking, and cut into slices.

mojito sorbet

zest and juice of 8–10 limes
  (you need 225ml lime juice)
175g white caster sugar
juice of 1 large lemon
100ml white rum
15 large young mint leaves, very
  finely chopped

To serve
mint leaves

What can I say – it's my favourite drink and now I've made it into a pudding! Don't be tempted to add more alcohol as it will take forever to freeze (or, depending on how much you've added, it won't freeze at all!)

Makes 675ml (enough for 4)

Put the lime zest and sugar into a pan with 150ml water and heat gently until dissolved, then cool for 5 minutes. Meanwhile, juice the limes and lemon and pour into a jug. Add the sugar syrup, rum and the mint and stir.

(**F**) Pour into a 1-litre container (a tall container is best if you have one; you can then just put a stick blender in to whizz it halfway through) and freeze for 4–5 hours, or until semi-frozen. Whizz with a stick blender or beat with a fork to break up the ice crystals. Return to the freezer. If possible, beat it again – the more you do, the finer the sorbet will be. Freeze again until frozen.

(**S**) Remove the sorbet from the freezer just before you want to use it and serve in little glasses, topped with some extra mint.

pavlova with pomegranates and raspberries

175ml egg white (about 4 large eggs, but make sure to measure)
350g golden caster sugar
2 teaspoons cornflour
1 teaspoon white wine vinegar

To serve
240g pomegranate seeds (about 4 fresh pomegranates)
300g raspberries, fresh or frozen
2 tablespoons caster sugar
300ml double cream

A billowy pavlova topped with ripe glistening fruits never fails to impress and, what's more, it's a heavenly combination to eat, too! It's definitely best to cook it in a conventional oven, as the fan seems to affect the texture and make it slightly less marshmallowy. Using frozen raspberries for this is ideal, as they defrost very quickly on the top and they add a burst of summer flavour to a winter menu. You can remove the seeds from fresh pomegranates instead of buying a pack of pomegranate seeds if you prefer – cheaper but a little more time consuming. The golden caster sugar gives the pavlova a more caramel colour.

Serves 6

Preheat the oven to 160°C/150°C fan/gas mark 3 (use conventional rather than fan if you can). Draw a 23cm-diameter circle on a sheet of greaseproof paper, then place the sheet on a large baking tray.

In a large bowl, using a hand-held electric whisk, whisk the egg whites on maximum speed until they form shiny stiff peaks. Add 6 teaspoons of the sugar, one straight after the other. Then, with the whisk still beating, add a further 2 teaspoons every 10 seconds until it is all incorporated. Sprinkle over the cornflour and vinegar and fold in using a large metal spoon.

Spoon the mixture into the centre of the greaseproof paper circle and spread out, levelling the centre and building up the sides to form peaks or swirls.

As soon as you place the pavlova into the oven, reduce the oven temperature to 150°C/140°C fan/gas mark 2 and bake for 1 hour. Turn off the oven and let the meringue cool completely while still in the oven, with the door ajar.

(F) Open freeze on the baking tray, then, if you need to, carefully transfer to a container or bag and cover before refreezing.

(D) Remove from the freezer 2 hours before you want to use it and defrost at room temperature.

(**S**) While the meringue defrosts, put half the pomegranate seeds and 75g of the raspberries into a pan with 2 tablespoons water. Simmer until the raspberries are softened and the mix is a little syrupy. Stir in the caster sugar then strain the mixture through a sieve and reserve the sauce. (You can do this ahead and keep in the fridge.) In a bowl, whip the cream and spread over the meringue. Scatter the remaining pomegranate seeds and raspberries over the top. Drizzle over the sauce and serve (or serve the sauce in a jug to hand around, if you prefer).

Variations:

Pavlova with strawberries and passion fruit – Make, freeze and defrost the pavlova following the recipe above and fill with 300ml whipped double cream. Scatter over 400g strawberries, halved if large, and the seeds from 2 passion fruit. Decorate with edible flowers, such as rose petals or pansies, if you wish.

Chocolate pavlova – You must use a standard cocoa for this rather than an upmarket one with a higher fat content, otherwise the mixture collapses. Add 1¹/₂ tablespoons of cocoa along with the sugar when making the pavlova.

Individual meringues – To make meringues rather than a pavlova, follow the pavlova recipe but reduce the quantity of sugar to 250g and omit the cornflour and vinegar. Spoon the mixture in 15–20 large, well-spaced dollops onto 2 baking trays lined with greaseproof paper. Bake at 110°C/100°C fan/gas mark ¹/₄ for 1 hour 20 minutes, or until the meringue bases are crisp and sound hollow when tapped gently. Leave to cool on their trays before placing in a container and freezing.

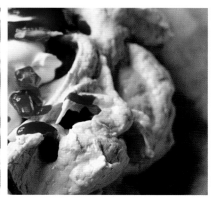

fruit cage puddings

200g redcurrants
200g blackcurrants
350g raspberries
75g golden caster sugar
1¹/₂ tablespoons crème de cassis
200g strawberries
8–10 medium slices white bread, one
    day old and crusts removed

To serve
whipped cream

My wonderful grandmother Sybil made summer puddings for us when
we were children – most, if not all, of the fruit coming from her garden.
I've renamed them fruit cage puddings as I have such happy memories of
her picking mountains of raspberries in the fruit cage they had. I've made
individual puddings as I think they look so dainty on a plate.

Makes 6

You will need 6 x 200ml dariole moulds

Put the redcurrants, blackcurrants and half the raspberries into a pan with
the sugar and crème de cassis and heat gently until the fruit begins to shine
and release its juice. Cook for a further 5 minutes or so, until you have a good
amount of liquid in the pan but the fruit still retains some texture.

Roll out the slices of bread using a rolling pin to stretch them and make
them a bit thinner. Using a cutter of the same diameter as the base of your
moulds, cut out 12 rounds. Cut the remaining bread slices into strips that
will fit around the insides of your moulds, just reaching the top. Dip one
side of each piece of bread into the fruit juices in the pan and fit the rounds
into the bottom and the strips around the inside of the moulds, fruity side
outwards, leaving 6 soaked rounds on a plate.

Add the remaining raspberries and strawberries to the pan, give them a stir,
then divide the fruit and remaining juices between the moulds. Top each
mould with a round of soaked bread (fruity side upwards) and cover the
moulds with cling film.

(**F**) Leave in the fridge for an hour, then cover each mould with foil and
transfer to the freezer.

(**D**) Leave at room temperature for about 4–6 hours.

(**S**) Turn the moulds out onto plates and serve with whipped cream.

flavoured vodkas

I am wondering whether my brother has set up a vodka factory from his home, and whether that's legal! I asked him to kindly investigate some interesting flavours of vodka, as he is a bit of a magician when it comes to experimenting with recipes and cocktails. Anyway, a few weeks later and here they are. All are totally delicious – and all deadly after dinner! They can also all can be stored in the freezer.

pomegranate vodka

Extract the seeds from a pomegranate by cutting in half, holding the cut side in the hollow of your hand and whacking the back with a rolling pin, then add the seeds to 500ml of vodka and steep for 12 hours. The vodka will go pinkish and take on some of the flavour. Drink as a shot with a few of the frozen seeds in each glass to crunch up as you drink.

strawberry and rosewater vodka

Cut 250g ripe strawberries into pieces small enough to fit through the neck of the vodka bottle. Add to 500ml of vodka, then add 2–4 teaspoons of rosewater and 50ml gomme or sugar syrup. Allow to steep for 24 hours then strain out the strawberries and place in the freezer. The vodka will be pink.

thai fire vodka

Score 1 lemongrass stick and 1 green chilli with a knife lengthways (but do not cut in half). Add to a 500ml bottle of vodka with a 2.5cm piece of fresh ginger or galangal, cut into lengths, and 10 fresh or 5 dried lime leaves, torn. Steep for 12 hours. Store in the freezer. This makes an amazing Bloody Mary and also works well layered with coconut milk in a shot glass.

speedy dishwasher chocolate and mint vodka

Smash up 100g 70% dark chocolate and feed it into a bottle containing 400ml vodka. Screw on the cap tightly and place in the dishwasher on a hot cycle. When it's finished, add 2–3 teaspoons good-quality mint extract to taste. Shake, cool and put in the freezer to chill. This recipe also works very well with the zest of 1 orange to replace the mint, or half a deseeded scored red chilli. And for those with a sweeter chocolate tooth, this method also works brilliantly with chopped up Mars Bars.

lollies

about 400ml–600ml fruit juice
(buy a variety of colours to make
stripy lollies, see opposite)

To serve (optional)
200g plain, milk or white chocolate
coloured sugar strands, stars or
chocolate sprinkles

I can never quite work out whether my son is eating something healthy
or frightful as he returns from a visit to our local shop munching a fruit-
flavoured lolly shaped like a cartoon character. I am now trying to make
lollies myself, where possible using some of the fabulous fruit juices and
smoothies available. If you have time, make them stripy or decorate them
with sprinkles; if not, just keep them simple. Getting the chocolate on can
be messy, but it is a fun activity for children.

Makes about 4 (depending on the size of your lolly moulds)

You will need 4 plastic lolly moulds with their plastic lids with sticks
attached (or wooden sticks if you prefer the old-fashioned look).

Pour the fruit juice into the lolly moulds until it reaches one third of the
way up, then freeze until just set. Once frozen, pour in juice of a contrasting
colour, then freeze again. When this second layer is semi-frozen, push in the
sticks, top up with a third flavour/colour and refreeze until solid. (You can
add as many stripes and refreeze as many times as you like, but it's best to
push the sticks in when the second layer is still semi-frozen to ensure they
are well secured.)

You can either serve the lollies as they are or decorate them with chocolate
and sprinkles. The easiest method I have found is to melt the chocolate in a
heatproof bowl over a pan of barely simmering water (or in the microwave),
then, using a spoon, drizzle a small amount of chocolate over the end of the
unmoulded completely frozen lolly and sprinkle with sugar strands. Rest
the lolly in the freezer – on a special lolly holder if you have one so that the
chocolate ends don't get smudged – and refreeze until solid.

treacle, orange and walnut tart

450g golden syrup (heat the jar/tin in some hot water to loosen the syrup first)

150g crustless white Breadcrumbs (see page 23, direct from the freezer is fine)

zest and juice of 1/2 orange

4 tablespoons double cream

1 egg, beaten

2 x 20cm blind-baked sweet pastry cases

100g packet walnut pieces

I make two of these tarts at a time to avoid wastage as one uses only half an egg, half a bag of walnuts and a quarter of an orange. I've made life easy and used ready-made and baked sweet pastry cases, but if you like, you can make your own pastry (see page 28), or buy a fresh block of pastry, line a couple of flan tins and blind bake the tart cases yourself (see page 144).

Makes 2 tarts, each serving 6

Preheat the oven to 190°C/180°C fan/gas mark 5. Pour the syrup into a smallish pan and melt over a low heat. Remove the pan from the heat and add the breadcrumbs, orange zest and juice, double cream and egg and stir to combine. Pour into the pastry cases and scatter with the walnut pieces. Bake for 20 minutes, then cool.

(F) Ideally, leave in the flan tin or foil tart case to freeze, but if you need to, once cool, you can carefully remove the tart before covering and freezing.

(R) To reheat from frozen, put into a preheated oven at 190°C/180°C fan/gas mark 5 for 15–20 minutes, or until piping hot. If defrosted, cook at 150°C/140°C fan/gas mark 2 for 25 minutes. Cover with foil if the pastry begins to look too dark.

late summer frangipane tart

flour, for dusting
350g (1/3 quantity) Sweet Pastry
  (see page 28)
175g butter, softened
175g ground almonds
150g caster sugar
3 large eggs
200g raspberries or blackberries or a
  mix of both, frozen or fresh
2 tablespoons flaked almonds

This is the perfect prepare-ahead tart: it is stylish, light enough for a dinner party (you can make it in individual cases if you like) and comforting enough to end a Sunday lunch party, too. Using frozen berries means you can enjoy it all year round.

Serves 6–8

If using frozen fruits, remove them from the freezer so that they can begin to defrost while you prepare the pastry. Preheat the oven to 190°C/180°C fan/gas mark 5.

On a floured surface, roll out the pastry and use it to line a 24cm-diameter x 2.5cm-deep loose-bottomed flan tin. Scrunch up a piece of greaseproof paper (it makes it easier to fit in the creases) and spread out over the pastry. Fill with baking beans. Bake for 15 minutes. Remove the paper and beans from the pastry case and return it to the oven for a further 5 minutes, or until the base has dried out. Then remove from the oven and leave to cool.

Put the butter, almonds, sugar and eggs into a food-processor and blitz for 20 seconds or so until combined and creamy. Spoon over the pastry base and top with the berries and flaked almonds. Bake for 40 minutes, or until evenly golden. Cool.

(**F**) Open freeze in its tin, then transfer to a bag and refreeze.

(**D**) Leave for about 2–4 hours at room temperature.

(**R**) Place in a preheated oven at 180°C/160°C fan/gas mark 4 for 10–15 minutes.

sticky banana apple puddings with toffee sauce

40g pecan nuts

2 very ripe bananas (blackened is best)

2 large eggs

1 1/2 tablespoons full-fat natural yogurt

1 x 150g (small) cooking apple, peeled, cored and grated

50g sultanas

85g butter, melted

110g light muscovado sugar

1/2 teaspoon ground cinnamon

185g self-raising flour

1 1/2 level teaspoons baking powder

3/4 teaspoon bicarbonate of soda

For the toffee sauce

175g light muscovado sugar

50g butter

300ml double cream

An alternative version of the pudding we all know and love, this has a hint of healthiness about it until you drown it in the toffee sauce!

You will need 8 x 200ml dariole moulds or mini pudding basins.

Preheat the oven to 180°C/160°C fan/gas mark 4. Grease the dariole moulds or mini pudding basins.

Scatter the pecan nuts on a baking tray and toast for about 5 minutes in the oven. Remove to a board and, when cool, roughly chop.

Using a fork, mash the bananas in a large bowl. Add the eggs, yogurt, grated apple, chopped nuts, sultanas, melted butter, sugar and cinnamon and mix together using the fork until thoroughly combined. Sift over the flour, baking powder and bicarbonate of soda and fold in gently, until only just combined, using a large metal spoon. Divide between the moulds and bake for 20–30 minutes, or until brown and cooked through. (Insert a skewer into the middle of one of the cakes to see if it comes out clean. If there's cake stuck to it, put it back in for a few more minutes.) Leave to cool slightly while you make the toffee sauce.

Put the sugar and butter into a pan over a low heat and stir until dissolved. Add the cream and simmer for 2–3 minutes until richly coloured. Remove from the heat and pour into a container. When the cakes are done, let them cool in their tins slightly then remove them by sliding a knife around the edges and transfer them to a wire rack to cool completely.

(**F**) Open freeze the cakes, then put them in bags, label and refreeze. Freeze the sauce in the container, covered.

(**D**) Leave for about 4–5 hours at room temperature.

(**R**) Warm the sauce slightly in a pan or the microwave, then pour half into the base of a baking dish. Sit the puddings on top and spoon over the remaining sauce. Cover with foil and bake in a preheated oven at 180°C/160°C fan/gas mark 4 for 15 minutes, or until piping hot and bubbling.

blackberry and apple crumble

25g butter

500g frozen cooking apple slices (or 3 medium cooking apples, cored, peeled and sliced)

3 tablespoons Demerara sugar

225g blackberries, fresh or frozen

4–6 handfuls Oaty Crumble Mix (see page 147), or enough to completely cover the fruit

To serve
ice cream

Just double the quantities and use a bigger dish for larger numbers, cooking for a little longer. If using your own frozen apple slices, you will probably need to defrost them slightly first as they can form a clump!

Serves 4

Preheat the oven to 180°C/160°C fan/gas mark 4.

Melt the butter in a saucepan and add the apples. Toss together for 2–3 minutes over the heat, then sprinkle in the sugar and add the frozen berries (if using fresh berries, add them right at the end of cooking). Stir over the heat until the blackberries are just beginning to turn the apples pinkish, then pour into a baking dish, patting down to fill in any gaps. Scatter over the crumble mix and bake for 30–40 minutes, or until golden and bubbling. Serve with ice cream.

Variations:

Summer berry – Use a mixture of different summer berries, frozen or fresh, in place of the blackberries. Or use 800g mixed berries on their own, and reduce the sugar to 1^1/$_2$ tablespoons. Soften the berries in a pan until they start to release their juice.

Raspberry and apple – Use frozen or fresh raspberries in place of the blackberries.

Rhubarb – Substitute the apple and blackberries with 600g frozen or fresh rhubarb chunks.

Apricot and apple – Use a tin of apricots in natural juice in place of the blackberries. Add the apricots, along with about half of their juice, to the apples after you have softened and sweetened them.

babies and children

feeding babies and toddlers

This will, I hope, make weaning and feeding babies and toddlers easier for busy parents. Weaning should be an exciting time, but as you may never have made purées before and you will want to make sure you are doing it right, it can feel like the pressure is on. The best advice is to keep it simple. And remember that a baby has never tasted apple or carrot before, so although it seems rather basic to us, it's a whole new world of taste for them and it might take a few attempts before your baby enjoys it.

This is where a freezer is a life-saver if you are a new parent: it enables you to make batches of different purées and freeze them in ice-cube trays, then introduce them slowly, rather than spending hours in the kitchen lovingly preparing something, only to have to throw it away when your child rejects it! A microwave is also a great help, if you use one, as is a stick blender.

You will want to wean your baby your own way, and every child is different, so I'm not going to attempt to give serving amounts or a routine for when to introduce new flavours. I haven't included everything as there's not enough space, and, in any case, I am sure you can work out how to boil a carrot or mash a banana! However, the first-stage combinations that follow have all been favourites with my children and hopefully will provide some inspiration for you too.

I have also included some easy-to-freeze dishes, such as Cauliflower Cheese and Pizza, that are suitable for toddlers but that I hope will be loved by all the family. Conversely, many of the recipes throughout the rest of book are also very baby and toddler friendly. You may just want to adjust the quantities of salt and sugar in the recipes if you are feeding young children.

first stages purées

apple and pear purée

2 eating apples, such as Braeburn
2 ripe pears (3 if small)

This was the first thing I introduced with both my children. You can mix it with a little baby rice to mellow the flavour a little.

Makes approx 20 cubes

Peel and core the fruits, then slice into a pan or microwaveable bowl. Add a tiny dash of water, then simmer gently for 5–8 minutes, or steam, until the fruits are soft. Alternatively cover the bowl with cling film, pierce a few times and microwave for 4–8 minutes, or until soft and mushy. Purée.

(**F**) Spoon the purée into ice-cube trays and leave to cool then freeze. Once frozen, transfer the cubes into a labelled freezer bag.

(**S**) Defrost, or warm through from frozen if you like.

pear and mango purée

2 ripe pears (3 if small)
2 ripe mangoes

This purée is uncooked, so ideal for a last-minute quick pudding.

Makes approx 20 cubes

Peel the fruits and slice into a bowl. Purée until smooth.

(**F**) Spoon the purée into ice-cube trays and leave to cool, then freeze. Once frozen, transfer the cubes into a labelled freezer bag.

(**S**) Defrost, or warm through from frozen if you like.

apple and blackberry purée

2 eating apples, such as Braeburn
150g blackberries

This one goes well with some baby rice or, when your baby is a little older, with some creamy rice pudding or custard mixed in. Soft rice is an ideal first texture.

Makes approx 20 cubes

Peel the apples, quarter and core, then slice into a pan or bowl. Add the blackberries and a dash of water, then simmer gently for 5–8 minutes until soft. Alternatively cover the bowl with cling film, pierce a few times and microwave for 4–6 minutes, or until soft (watch it though as it does have a tendency to boil over). Purée.

(**F**) Spoon the purée into ice-cube trays and leave to cool, then freeze. Once frozen, transfer the cubes into a labelled freezer bag.

(**S**) Defrost, or warm through from frozen if you like.

red pepper and sweet potato purée

350g sweet potato, peeled and cut
   into chunks
100g fresh or frozen sliced mixed
   peppers or 100g red pepper,
   deseeded and chopped
splash of cooking water, or some milk
   and a knob of butter if your baby is
   at this stage

Using frozen pepper slices is just as nutritious and a quick way to rustle up a batch of purée.

Makes approx 12 cubes

Boil the sweet potato for 15 minutes, then add the frozen pepper, bring back to the boil and continue to cook for 5 minutes. (If you are using fresh pepper, add it 5 minutes earlier and make sure it is soft before draining.) Drain, reserving a little of the cooking water if needed, and blend until puréed completely (make sure there are no stray bits of pepper skin as babies don't really like this!). Stir in milk and butter or a splash of the cooking water to loosen if necessary.

(**F**) Spoon into ice-cube trays, cool and freeze, then transfer to a freezer bag, label and refreeze.

(**S**) Reheat. You can cook from frozen if you like.

beetroot and carrot purée

200g carrots, peeled and cut into chunks
3 peeled, cooked beetroot, cut into chunks
4 tablespoons milk or cooking water

My daughter Jemima loves this as it's so sweet. The beetroot also turns the purée the most stunning vivid pink! I often combine it with mashed potato. If your baby is at the right stage, you can also cook the vegetables in chicken stock for more flavour. Use fresh cooked beetroot, if you have some to hand (boil the unpeeled beets for about 25 minutes, or until soft, then peel), or precooked beetroot in natural juice.

Makes approx 14 cubes

Boil the carrots in water for about 15 minutes, or until tender.
Drain, reserving some of the cooking water, then add the beetroot and purée.
Add the milk or cooking water to loosen.

(F) Spoon the purée into ice-cube trays and leave to cool, then freeze. Once frozen, transfer the cubes into a labelled freezer bag.

(S) Reheat. You can cook from frozen if you like.

pizza

500g pack of ciabatta bread mix

1 tablespoon olive oil (or quantity specified in bread mix), plus 2 tablespoons for the top

flour, for dusting

4–5 heaped tablespoons All-purpose Tomato Sauce (see page 33), or a good-quality shop-bought tomato sauce

1 teaspoon dried oregano

2 x 125g packs of mozzarella balls, drained

Topping suggestions:

My children's favourite – ham, sweetcorn, chopped pepper, olives and courgette

Quattro Stagioni – artichokes, black olives, sliced mushrooms and strips of ham

Fiery – crushed chilli flakes, pepperoni slices and pepper strips

Veggie – roasted pepper strips, blanched asparagus spears and finely sliced courgette

I have to thank my great mate Kate Titford for opening my eyes to pizza making – using an Italian bread mix as a base suddenly transformed what I used to think was always a rather spongey end result into seriously good crispy pizza. My children adore sprinkling on their own toppings, and these are perfect for that – especially to make ahead for a children's party. Make smaller circles if you'd like them to have one each. However, they are also a huge temptation on a Sunday evening when you get the munchies!

Makes 2 large pizzas, each big enough to serve 2–3 adults or about 4 children

In a bowl, mix the bread mix according to the pack instructions. (The one I use says to mix in 350ml lukewarm water and knead for 5 minutes, then add a tablespoon of olive oil and knead for a further minute, but yours might vary slightly.) Once you have a mixed and kneaded ball of dough, and it no longer feels sticky, cut it into 2 equal pieces and put into a large baking dish, covered in cling film. Leave in a warm place (an airing cupboard, an oven that has been turned off but is still warm, or on top of the boiler) for about 30 minutes, or until it has doubled in size.

Remove one of the balls of dough from the dish and place it onto a floured work surface. Using your hand, covered in a little flour, knead the dough on the work surface to remove the air, reshape to a circle and roll out thinly to a larger circle of approximately 30–35cm diameter. Put onto a flat non-stick baking tray. Repeat with the other dough ball and lay out onto another tray.

Spoon 2–3 tablespoons of tomato sauce into the middle of each of the pizzas and spread nearly to the edges. Sprinkle each pizza with 1/2 teaspoon oregano and a good grinding of pepper. Then tear each mozzarella ball into pieces, dry off with a piece of kitchen paper and scatter over each pizza.

(F) Open freeze on the baking trays, then remove to a bag or stack between layers of greaseproof paper and cover tightly with cling film.

(D) For best results, defrost for 3–4 hours at room temperature, however you can cook from frozen if you don't have time – just don't overload with toppings or the centre will be a bit soggy.

(C) Preheat the oven to 220°C/200°C fan/gas mark 7 and place 2 baking trays into the oven at the same time. Top the pizzas with the toppings of your choice, then drizzle with a tablespoon or so of extra virgin olive oil. Transfer to the preheated baking trays and bake for 10–15 minutes if defrosted or 15–20 minutes from frozen.

acknowledgements

I'm so incredibly grateful to all my family and friends who have been kind enough to test recipes from the book to make sure they are in tip-top shape:

Katherine Coltart, Simon and Ness Baker, Harry Cox, Mel Clegg, Ems Bray, Mrs Edgecombe, Gemma Pearce, Judy Snell, Andrea Eles, Isabel Sandison, Katie James, Marcia Ritchie, Clare Evelyn, Tania MacCallum, Lesley Sandison, Soph Martin, Jane Brooke, Els Rooth, Anna Greenhalgh, Alex Nolon, Claire Davies, Anna Broome, Jane Wiggs, Lucy Urquhart, Rebecca Bone, Ali Palmer, Katherine McNamara, Katie Callard, Debbie Sandison and Gill Head. You are all wonderful!

Yet again, extra special thanks go to my brother, mother and mother-in-law, all of whom have been happy to ponder book ideas over the phone, share their recipes and drop everything to help with both cooking and child minding – big, big thanks to you!

Thanks also to Georgie Sangiorgio and Claire Davies, who worked their way through all the recipes, checking the copy made sense, giving feedback and generally getting me organised!

Catharine, Estella, Jenny, Victoria, Emma and the rest of the team at Kyle Cathie are all supreme champions as far as I'm concerned. They have put up with many a weird question and whim without the slightest flicker of annoyance, throughout the entire process of making this book, as with my previous one!

Kyle, I am hugely grateful to you for giving me this incredible opportunity – I hope I do you proud.

Last, but not least, thanks to A, W and J, who have been encouraging, patient, supportive and in general just all-round superstars. Thanks for munching your way through the entire book, even when at early stages of testing! All I will say is, at least it's a bit more varied than jam!